DEAR SOS

◆◆◆

Favorite Restaurant Recipes
from the Los Angeles Times

by Rose Dosti

Los Angeles, California

Los Angeles Times

Publisher: John P. Puerner
Editor: John S. Carroll

Los Angeles Times
BOOKS

Book Development General Manager: Carla Lazzareschi
Editor: Patricia Connell
Design: Moritz Design
Nutritional Analysis: Bruce Henstell
ISBN 1-883792-60-6
© Los Angeles Times 2001
Published by the Los Angeles Times
202 W. 1st Street, Los Angeles, California 90012
First printing June 2001
Printed in the U.S.A.

CONTENTS

◆◆◆

To the faithful readers of "Culinary SOS"

whose requests have been a great source of joy

to millions over the last 50 years.

INTRODUCTION

♦♦♦

This is the third *Dear SOS* cookbook based exclusively on recipes appearing in the "Culinary SOS" column, one of the nation's most popular recipe-request columns, which has been appearing in the *Los Angeles Times* food section for nearly a half century.

Dear SOS: Thirty Years of Recipe Requests to the Los Angeles Times (1994), an all-category recipe book, was followed in 1996 by *Dear SOS Desserts*, a subject dear to the hearts of many column readers. Both books contain recipes that have been time-tested favorites throughout the column's long history. Popular and oft-requested recipes not found in one volume will likely appear in another.

Now it's time to produce another *Dear SOS* that focuses exclusively on restaurant dishes, our readers' most frequently requested recipes of all types. Restaurant recipes, in fact, set the tone for the way many Americans cook and dine today. One reason is that as more and more families eat out, they are increasingly inspired to re-create the new and exciting dishes they've sampled. Further, while home cooking was once a life skill, today it has become a hobby for both men and women. In fact, more men request "Culinary SOS" recipes today than ever before.

In the old days in Los Angeles—we're talking early 1950s—average restaurant dining was about as exciting as Sunday dinner with the Clampetts. Except for a handful of legendary restaurants—Scandia, Perino's, Au Petit Jean, Chasen's and the Cock n' Bull, among others—the restaurant scene was, shall we say, provincial.

Given such a history, one might think restaurant recipes rarely appeared in "Culinary SOS." Not so. They have been featured in the column since its inception in the early 1950s, when Anita Bennett wrote it for the *Daily Mirror* before it was merged in 1961 with the *Los Angeles Times*. The column ran for a few years under Bennett's name and then was taken over in the late 1960s by Cecil Fleming, a *Times* home economist. (I was assigned the column several years later and have been writing it ever since.)

The recipes appearing in the column's early days were mainly from high-profile restaurants with a few more humble establishments, such as Tick Tock, Clifton's Cafeteria, Robaire's and Maison Gerard, thrown in for good measure. Recipes from these restaurants are popular to this day.

"Culinary SOS," which continues to run weekly, received a surge in demand for restaurant recipes in the early 1980s when Los Angeles witnessed an explosion of restaurants rivaling those in San Francisco and New York. Several factors were responsible for the sudden upturn. A steady improvement in the global economy brought an influx of chefs from Europe and Asia—especially France, Italy, Japan and Taiwan—to our shores. A significant wave of immigrants from Thailand, Vietnam, Korea, Japan and Taiwan, as well as from throughout Central and South America, also brought new culinary vision to the restaurant scene. Americans now enjoy Korean bulgogi, Japanese sukiyaki and sushi and Thailand's pad Thai as much as Italian pasta and risotto and fanciful nouvelle cuisine from France. New technologies brought products to market overnight. Seafoods rarely seen in Los Angeles before, such as tiger shrimp from Thailand, green mussels from New Zealand, mullet from the Red Sea and fish from the Adriatic, became standard fare in restaurants. With their appetites awakened to new and different foods, diners wanted to learn how to make these dishes at home. By the late 1980s, restaurant recipes were far more sought after than Aunt Jenny's favorite rice pudding or Mom's apple crisp, and today our mailbag—or should I say e-mail file—is almost exclusively filled with requests for restaurant recipes.

But make no mistake; restaurant recipes are a greater challenge to the everyday cook than recipes developed strictly for home use. Professional chefs are accustomed to working with several pans simultaneously and reaching for ingredients that have been prepared in advance. They are blessed with a stockpot at the ready for flavoring sauces, top-of-the-line commercial equipment, small armies of assistants and countertop space galore.

Home cooking, on the other hand, relies on a one-step-at-a-time approach. As a result, each restaurant recipe we receive requires alteration and translation to adapt it for the home cook. My hat goes off to the *Times'* test kitchen staff—Donna Deane, Mayi Brady and student apprentices from various cooking schools around the country who spend a term in our kitchen testing recipes. We also credit all previous kitchen staffers who labored over our restaurant recipes.

One of a food writer's greatest pleasures and learning experiences is visiting ethnic food stores. We look around, read labels, ask questions of the clerk and learn a great deal. We urge you to do the same when you are confronted with unfamiliar ingredients.

Each of the recipes in this book includes a nutrient analysis. But don't be dissuaded from preparing a dish just because of its high calorie or fat content. Recipes, as Julia Child often points out, are not just about calories and fat. They are meant to provide shared pleasure. If calories and fat are a concern, simply limit the amount you eat.

We have constructed the chapters according to the popularity of the subject. The soup, vegetable, meat and dessert chapters are the largest because readers request more of these recipes than other dishes. We've listed the recipes in the beginning of each chapter to make it easier to find what you're looking for. You can create a menu simply by scanning the lists.

Most important, we want you to enjoy every minute you spend reading or cooking from these recipes. They are meant to please, entertain and instruct. Enjoy.

Rose Dosti
June 2001

APPETIZERS

◆◆◆

A few decades ago, most restaurants, other than ethnic establishments, listed only one or two appetizers on their menu. Today there are almost as many appetizers on restaurant menus as there are main courses—sometimes even more.

The reason is simple. Californians—and perhaps most Americans today —adore appetizers. Contemporary eating styles make it entirely acceptable for a diner to order a complete meal from the appetizer menu. Today's diners have been introduced to a wide variety of cuisines and appreciate more than ever their different tastes and styles. How can you resist dipping crusty bread in the olive puree that is served as an appetizer in many Italian restaurants? How can you pass up crisp Buffalo wings, or bits of Thai-flavored chicken or meat on skewers ready to dip in a peanut sauce?

But don't worry. These exciting new dishes haven't elbowed out the familiar and popular dips and nibbles. They are here, too.

Pancetta Cheese Balls ◆ Ca'Brea

Olive Puree ◆ I Cugini

Guacamole ◆ Bryant Park Grille

Spinach and Artichoke Dip ◆ Knott's Berry Farm

Hot Crab Dip ◆ Palomino

Checca Appetizer ◆ Pane Caldo

Stuffed Mushrooms ◆ Gene Autry Museum of Western Heritage

Deviled Beef Ribs with Mustard Sauce ◆ Waldorf Astoria

Buffalo Wings ◆ Elephant Bar

Satays with Peanut Sauce ◆ Siamese Princess

Ahi Carpaccio ◆ Michael's

Maryland Crab Cakes ◆ Grill at Park Circle

Oysters Rockefeller ◆ Oysters

Shrimp Cocktail ◆ Las Casuelas Terraza

Salmon Tartare ◆ L'Ermitage

Gravad Lax ◆ Scandia

Peppered Pecans ◆ Gumbo Pot

PANCETTA CHEESE BALLS

Ca'Brea, Hollywood

Serve as bite-size snacks to pass with drinks, or scatter over a wilted spinach salad for lunch.

10 ounces goat cheese
2 ounces dry-type farmer cheese or ricotta cheese
8 ounces pancetta, prosciutto or bacon, sliced paper thin
2 tablespoons olive oil
1 clove garlic, minced

Mix goat cheese with farmer cheese until well blended. Form into 1- to 1 1/2-inch balls. Wrap with pancetta until completely covered. Chill.

Arrange pancetta appetizers on broiler pan and broil 3 to 4 inches from heat source until pancetta is crisp and cheese is somewhat melted. Serve on wooden picks.

❖ *Chef's Tip*: To make a spinach salad, sauté 1 pound spinach, washed and patted dry, in 1/4 cup olive oil just until wilted. Arrange as a bed for the pancetta cheese balls.

◆◆◆

12 appetizer or 8 main course servings. Each of 12 servings contains about: 122 calories; 332 mg sodium; 23 mg cholesterol; 9 grams fat; 1 gram carbohydrate; 8 grams protein; 0.01 gram fiber.

OLIVE PUREE

I Cugini, Santa Monica

This spread, served with slices of crusty bread, is more a method than a recipe. It is one used by many Italian restaurants.

1 1/2 cups Kalamata olives, drained and pitted
2 to 3 tablespoons extra-virgin olive oil

Chop olives in food processor until ground to medium-fine consistency. Moisten with enough olive oil to make a spreadable mixture. (The amount of oil used will vary with the type of olives, as some contain more oil than others.)

Store spread in refrigerator; stir before serving. Use as spread for bread, toast or crackers.

1/2 cup. Each tablespoon contains about: 88 calories; 568 mg sodium; 0 cholesterol; 10 grams fat; 2 grams carbohydrate; trace protein; 0.66 gram fiber.

GUACAMOLE

Bryant Park Grille, New York City

The ingredients in this quite standard creamy guacamole from New York City's Bryant Park Grille are nicely balanced. It's a great dip for Super Bowl time.

8 ripe Haas avocados
I red onion, diced
1/2 cup cilantro leaves, chopped
3 jalapeños, diced, with seeds
2 plum tomatoes, diced
Juice of 3 limes
Salt

Cut avocados in half. Remove seeds. Scoop out avocado flesh and place in wooden bowl. Mash with spoon until creamy and smooth. Fold in onion, cilantro, jalapeños, tomatoes and lime juice. Mix well. Season to taste with salt. Serve immediately.

◆◆◆

18 servings. Each serving contains about: 141 calories; 26 mg sodium; 0 cholesterol; 13 grams fat; 7 grams carbohydrate; 2 grams protein; 1.72 grams fiber.

SPINACH and ARTICHOKE DIP

Knott's Berry Farm, Buena Park

A reader pleaded with us to persuade Knott's Berry Farm to release its recipe for classic spinach dip. We succeeded.

8 ounces cream cheese
1/4 cup heavy whipping cream
1/2 cup mayonnaise
1/4 teaspoon garlic powder
1/2 teaspoon onion salt
1/2 cup shredded mozzarella cheese
6 ounces spinach, chopped
8 ounces cooked or canned artichoke hearts, quartered
Tortilla chips

Heat cream cheese, whipping cream, mayonnaise, garlic powder and onion salt in saucepan over low heat, stirring until smooth. Fold in mozzarella, spinach and artichoke hearts and cook over low heat until spinach is wilted, about 5 minutes. Serve hot with tortilla chips.

◆◆◆

3 cups. Each 1-tablespoon serving, without tortilla chips, contains about: 38 calories; 48 mg sodium; 6 mg cholesterol; 4 grams fat; 1 gram carbohydrate; 1 gram protein; 0.03 gram fiber.

HOT CRAB DIP
Palomino, Westwood

Palomino serves this topped with herbed bread crumbs and stuck with a wedge of herbed pizza crust. Herbed crackers can be used in lieu of pizza crust.

HERBED BREAD CRUMBS:
1/4 loaf day-old baguette
2 tablespoons butter, melted
I teaspoon minced garlic
1/4 teaspoon dried rosemary
1/4 teaspoon dried basil
1/4 teaspoon chopped fresh parsley
1/4 teaspoon chopped fresh thyme
1/4 teaspoon chopped fresh oregano
1/4 teaspoon chopped fresh marjoram

CRAB DIP:
I cup mayonnaise
2 packages (8 ounces each) frozen artichoke hearts, thawed and coarsely chopped
I 1/4 pounds cooked Dungeness crabmeat
1/2 small white onion, sliced paper thin
1/2 teaspoon salt
I ounce Parmesan cheese, grated
2 teaspoons lemon juice
Chopped fresh parsley

HERBED CRACKERS:
1/2 cup olive oil
2 teaspoons minced sun-dried tomatoes (not oil-packed)
I teaspoon mixed dried herbs, such as rosemary, basil, parsley, thyme, oregano, marjoram
36 water crackers

HERBED BREAD CRUMBS:

Cut baguette into 1-inch cubes. Place in food processor and grind to coarse (about 3/8-inch) crumbs; do not overprocess.

Combine bread crumbs, butter, garlic, rosemary, basil, parsley, thyme, oregano and marjoram. Mix until butter is evenly distributed and absorbed by bread crumbs.

CRAB DIP:

Preheat oven to 500 degrees. Combine mayonnaise, artichoke hearts, crabmeat, onion and salt. Mix well.

Spread crab mixture in 9-inch square casserole and top with Herbed Bread Crumbs and cheese. Bake until very hot and bubbly, 5 minutes. Drizzle lemon juice over top. Sprinkle with chopped parsley. Serve with plain or Herbed Crackers.

HERBED CRACKERS:

Combine olive oil, tomatoes and mixed herbs. Let stand several hours or overnight before using. Drizzle or brush over crackers just before serving.

5 cups dip. Each tablespoon, without crackers, contains about: 37 calories; 66 mg sodium; 4 mg cholesterol; 1 gram fat; 1 gram carbohydrate; 1 gram protein; 0.08 gram fiber.

36 crackers. Each cracker contains about: 52 calories; 62 mg sodium; 0 cholesterol; 4 grams fat; 4 grams carbohydrate; 1 gram protein; 0.02 gram fiber.

CHECCA APPETIZER

Pane Caldo, Los Angeles

Some restaurants pass this appetizer salad in a bowl to allow diners to spoon portions over warm toast; others serve the salad on toast before the meal arrives, as Pane Caldo did. You can sop up the juices at the bottom of the bowl with extra toast when the Checca is gone.

I pound ripe tomatoes, finely diced
3 fresh basil leaves, chopped
1/4 cup extra-virgin olive oil
2 cloves garlic, sliced
Salt, pepper
24 (2-inch-diameter) slices French baguette or Italian bread, toasted

Combine tomatoes and basil in bowl. Toss lightly. Add olive oil and garlic. Season to taste with salt and pepper. Toss just until tomatoes are evenly coated with oil. Cover and set aside 7 to 10 minutes. Serve over toast slices.

◆◆◆

2 cups or 24 appetizers. Each appetizer contains about: 124 calories; 194 mg sodium; 0 mg cholesterol; 3 grams fat; 21 grams carbohydrate; 4 grams protein; 1.21 grams fiber.

STUFFED MUSHROOMS

Golden Spur Cafe, Gene Autry Museum of Western Heritage, Los Angeles

Somerset Caterers, which operates the Golden Spur Cafe in the Gene Autry Museum, sent this stuffed mushroom recipe with a "howdy" and a "thank you, ma'am" for asking. Serve this as an appetizer or a vegetable side dish.

24 large white mushrooms
1/4 cup (1/2 stick) butter, melted
Salt, pepper
1/2 cup minced onion
1/2 cup minced shallots
3 tablespoons vegetable oil
2/3 cup Madeira
1/2 cup plain dry bread crumbs
2/3 cup grated Gruyère cheese
2/3 cup freshly grated Parmesan cheese
2/3 cup minced fresh parsley
1/3 cup (about) whipping cream

Remove stems from mushrooms. Mince stems and set aside. Arrange mushroom caps on baking sheet. Brush caps with melted butter and season with salt and pepper. Set aside.

Sauté onion and shallots in oil and any remaining butter in skillet over medium heat until tender but not browned, 3 to 4 minutes. Add minced mushroom stems. Raise heat to high and sauté until liquid is absorbed, 4 to 5 minutes. Add Madeira and bring to boil; boil until liquid evaporates. Cool.

Preheat oven to 375 degrees. Add bread crumbs, Gruyère and Parmesan cheeses and parsley to mushroom mixture. Add enough cream to bind mixture. Adjust seasoning. Spoon stuffing into mushroom caps. Bake until hot and bubbly, 10 to 12 minutes. Serve immediately.

8 servings. Each serving contains about: 264 calories; 335 mg sodium; 47 mg cholesterol; 21 grams fat; 9 grams carbohydrate; 9 grams protein; 0.38 gram fiber.

DEVILED BEEF RIBS with MUSTARD SAUCE

Waldorf Astoria, New York City

We love Waldorf Astoria recipes from our old files, not only for nostalgic reasons but also because they're great.

8 pounds beef ribs (from prime rib, about 2 racks)
Salt, pepper
4 tablespoons (about) virgin olive oil
I cup Dijon mustard
2 1/2 cups fine dry bread crumbs
1 1/4 cup veal or beef broth
1/2 cup Madeira
1/2 teaspoon cornstarch
1/2 teaspoon water
2 tablespoons butter

Preheat oven to 325 degrees. Lightly season ribs with salt and pepper. Place on baking tray and roast 1 1/2 hours. Let cool until easy to handle, about 15 minutes.

Combine 3 tablespoons olive oil and all but 3 tablespoons mustard, blending well. Separate beef into rib sections and coat lightly with mustard mixture. Dredge each piece in bread crumbs and place on baking tray.

Preheat oven to 375 degrees. Sprinkle ribs lightly with remaining olive oil. Bake until golden brown, about 10 to 15 minutes.

Combine broth and Madeira in skillet over medium heat. Cook until reduced by half. Combine cornstarch with water until smooth. Stir into sauce and cook until sauce coats back of spoon. Continue to simmer several minutes to blend flavors. Whisk in butter and reserved mustard. Stir until smooth. Serve sauce with ribs.

◆◆◆

6 servings. Each serving contains about: 704 calories; 1,631 mg sodium; 104 mg cholesterol; 47 grams fat; 25 grams carbohydrate; 29 grams protein; 0.10 gram fiber.

BUFFALO WINGS

Elephant Bar, Goleta

The Elephant Bar serves its Buffalo wings with Frank's Louisiana Hot Sauce and Grey Poupon Dijon mustard, but almost any Louisiana-style hot sauce or Dijon-style mustard may be used.

I cup hot sauce
3 tablespoons Dijon mustard
I tablespoon prepared horseradish with juice
1/4 cup (1/2 stick) butter, melted
24 chicken wings, about 4 1/2 pounds
Vegetable oil

Blend hot sauce, mustard and horseradish at low speed in blender. Slowly add melted butter, being sure butter is well incorporated into sauce mixture. If fat appears on surface, stop adding butter until all ingredients are thoroughly mixed. (Sauce can be stored in refrigerator up to 5 days.)

Preheat oven to 450 degrees. Bake chicken wings on oiled baking sheet until cooked through, 30 to 35 minutes. Remove wings from oven and drain off excess fat. Serve with dipping sauce.

◆◆◆

24 wings. Each wing, with I tablespoon sauce, contains about: 105 calories; 91 mg sodium; 32 mg cholesterol; 8 grams fat; 0 carbohydrate; 6 grams protein; 0.01 gram fiber.

SATAYS with PEANUT SAUCE

Siamese Princess, Hollywood

These satays from the former Siamese Princess make ideal holiday party appetizers because you can prepare them in advance and keep them refrigerated for up to 48 hours before grilling.

SATAYS:

1 pound chicken breasts or lean pork, beef or lamb, thinly sliced
3 cloves garlic, minced
1/2 onion, minced
2 teaspoons minced cilantro
1 tablespoon brown sugar
Juice of 1 lime
1 tablespoon nam pla (Thai fish sauce)
1 tablespoon vegetable oil

PEANUT SAUCE:

1/2 cup crunchy peanut butter
1 onion, minced
1 stalk lemongrass, minced
1 cup coconut milk
1 tablespoon brown sugar
1 teaspoon chili powder
1 tablespoon nam pla (Thai fish sauce)
1 tablespoon dark soy sauce

SATAYS:

Thread meat onto 16 12-inch bamboo skewers, allowing several slices on each skewer.

Combine garlic, onion, cilantro, brown sugar, lime juice, fish sauce and oil in bowl. Pour over skewers and marinate 1 hour. Grill skewers over medium coals or on broiler rack 3 inches from heat source until done as desired, turning skewers several times. Serve with Peanut Sauce.

PEANUT SAUCE:

Combine peanut butter, onion, lemongrass, coconut milk, brown sugar, chili powder, fish sauce and soy sauce in saucepan and bring to boil. Remove from heat. Pour into small bowls to serve as dipping sauce for skewers.

16 servings. Each serving, with 1 tablespoon Peanut Sauce, contains about: 121 calories; 196 mg sodium; 12 mg cholesterol; 8 grams fat; 5 grams carbohydrate; 8 grams protein; 0.83 gram fiber.

AHI CARPACCIO
Michael's, Santa Monica

Michael's uses truffle shavings as a garnish, but they can be omitted.

8 ounces fresh ahi tuna, sliced paper thin
Salt
Extra-virgin olive oil
White wine vinegar
Freshly cracked black pepper
1 bunch arugula or watercress
Freshly grated Parmesan cheese
1/2 to 1 white or black fresh or canned truffle, shaved (optional)

Arrange tuna in overlapping slices on platter or tray. Sprinkle with salt and drizzle with oil and vinegar to taste. Season with pepper. Surround tuna with wreath of arugula. Sprinkle with grated Parmesan cheese. Garnish with truffle shavings, if desired.

◆◆◆

4 appetizer servings. Each serving contains about: 143 calories; 374 mg sodium; 20 mg cholesterol; 10 grams fat; 1 gram carbohydrate; 12 grams protein; 0.07 gram fiber.

MARYLAND CRAB CAKES

Grill at Park Circle, Hagerstown, Maryland

The chef at Grill at Park Circle uses jumbo lump backfin crabmeat to make these authentic Maryland crab cakes. Most markets carry it. Old Bay Seasoning is preferred, but any seafood-poultry seasoning blend would work.

1 pound lump crabmeat, cleaned
1/4 cup fresh white bread crumbs, without crust
2 tablespoons low-fat mayonnaise
1 teaspoon Dijon mustard
1 egg, beaten
1 teaspoon seafood seasoning blend
Dash of Worcestershire sauce
Dash of hot pepper sauce
Juice of 1/2 lemon
Pinch of salt
White pepper

Gently toss crabmeat and bread crumbs together, being careful not to break up crabmeat.

Combine mayonnaise, mustard, egg, seafood seasoning, Worcestershire sauce, hot pepper sauce, lemon juice, salt and pepper in separate bowl and mix well.

Preheat oven to 400 degrees. Grease baking pan. Gently fold crabmeat mixture into sauce mixture until thoroughly mixed. Shape into 4 cakes. Bake on prepared pan until golden brown, 20 to 25 minutes. Serve hot.

4 crab cakes. Each cake contains about: 165 calories; 589 mg sodium; 72 mg cholesterol; 4 grams fat; 5 grams carbohydrate; 25 grams protein; 0.02 gram fiber.

OYSTERS ROCKEFELLER

Oysters Restaurant, Corona del Mar

This recipe uses Fanny Bay oysters from Washington state, but any medium-size oyster will do.

8 ounces applewood-smoked bacon, finely diced
4 cups packed finely chopped spinach leaves
Anisette or Pernod
1/4 cup lemon juice
Freshly grated Parmesan cheese
3/4 cup mayonnaise
I teaspoon freshly ground pepper
18 Fanny Bay oysters
Lemon wedges for garnish

Sauté bacon over medium heat until browned and crisp, 8 to 10 minutes. Remove from pan and drain on paper towels.

Combine bacon, spinach, 1/4 cup anisette, lemon juice, 3/4 cup Parmesan cheese, mayonnaise and pepper in large bowl. (Mixture may be refrigerated up to 3 days in airtight container.)

When ready to serve, preheat oven to 425 degrees. Shuck oysters and remove any shell fragments. Arrange oysters in shells on baking sheet. Drizzle each with about I teaspoon anisette and bake until oysters are cooked, about 5 minutes. Let cool about 15 minutes. Maintain oven temperature.

Spoon about 2 tablespoons spinach mixture over each oyster and bake until lightly browned and bubbling, 4 to 6 minutes. Garnish with additional freshly grated Parmesan cheese and lemon wedges.

◆◆◆

6 servings. Each serving contains about: 407 calories; 721 mg sodium; 59 mg cholesterol; 31 grams fat; 17 grams carbohydrate; 12 grams protein; 0.33 gram fiber.

SHRIMP COCKTAIL

Las Casuelas Terraza, Palm Springs

Here's an unusual treatment for shrimp cocktail from a popular Palm Springs restaurant.

3 tomatoes, diced
I cucumber, peeled, seeded and diced
I medium-size white onion, chopped
I small bunch cilantro, chopped
I can (I2 ounces) red chile sauce
I bottle (7 ounces) ketchup
Juice of I large lemon
I 1/2 teaspoons prepared horseradish
3/4 cup tomato juice
2 pounds raw shrimp

Combine tomatoes, cucumber, onion and cilantro in bowl.

In separate bowl, blend chile sauce, ketchup, lemon juice, horseradish and tomato juice.

Cook shrimp in pan of simmering water to cover just until shrimp turn pink. Drain, reserving I cup shrimp cooking broth. Peel and coarsely chop shrimp. Add reserved broth to tomato sauce mixture. Add shrimp and mix well. Chill. Serve in chilled cocktail glasses.

◆◆◆

8 servings. Each serving contains about: 158 calories; 631 mg sodium; 124 mg cholesterol; 2 grams fat; 17 grams carbohydrate; 18 grams protein; 1.05 grams fiber.

SALMON TARTARE

L'Ermitage, West Hollywood

L'Ermitage was probably one of the first establishments to put salmon tartare on the map. Even though the restaurant is gone, the recipe goes on and on.

9 ounces smoked salmon
2 tablespoons chopped onion
I tablespoon chopped capers
I tablespoon chopped fresh parsley
I tablespoon lemon juice
2 tablespoons sour cream
Toast points

   Finely chop smoked salmon with sharp knife. In large bowl combine salmon, onion, capers, parsley, lemon juice and sour cream and mix well. Serve with toast points.

◆◆◆

6 servings. Each serving contains about: 62 calories; 896 mg sodium; 12 mg cholesterol; 3 grams fat; I gram carbohydrate; 8 grams protein; 0.14 gram fiber.

GRAVAD LAX

Scandia, West Hollywood

If you've got the bagels, we've got the lox from fondly remembered Scandia.

GRAVAD LAX:

1 2-pound salmon fillet
3 tablespoons salt
3 tablespoons sugar
1 tablespoon crushed peppercorns
1/2 bunch fresh dill

MUSTARD-DILL SAUCE:

1/4 cup Dijon mustard
3 tablespoons sugar
2 tablespoons white wine vinegar
1 teaspoon dry mustard
1/3 cup vegetable oil
3 tablespoons chopped fresh dill

GRAVAD LAX:

Split salmon in half lengthwise, holding knife horizontally. Remove any bones. Combine salt, sugar and peppercorns. Rub half of spice mixture over one salmon half and place fish, skin side down, in baking dish. Spread dill over.

Rub other half of salmon with remaining spice mixture and place skin side up on first salmon half. Cover with foil. Place plate on top of fish and top with weight.

Refrigerate 48 hours. Turn fish every 12 hours, separating fillets slightly to baste.

When ready to serve, scrape away dill and seasonings. Place salmon pieces skin side down on cutting board. Cut diagonally in thin slices away from skin. Serve cold with Mustard-Dill Sauce.

MUSTARD-DILL SAUCE:

Combine mustard, sugar, vinegar and dry mustard. Slowly beat in oil until thick. Stir in dill. Chill. About 3/4 cup.

24 servings. Each serving, with sauce, contains about: 106 calories; 960 mg sodium; 19 mg cholesterol; 5 grams fat; 7 grams carbohydrate; 7 grams protein; 0.09 gram fiber.

PEPPERED PECANS
Gumbo Pot, Farmers Market, Hollywood

At the Gumbo Pot in Los Angeles' bustling Farmers Market, these spicy-sweet nuts are served on a fried chicken salad with creamy pecan dressing, but they are also great to pass with drinks.

$1/2$ cup sugar
I tablespoon kosher salt
I $1/2$ tablespoons freshly ground black pepper
4 ounces pecan halves

Mix sugar, salt and pepper. Set aside.

Heat cast iron skillet until hot enough to vaporize water. Shake pecans in skillet I minute to release oil. Lightly toast until fragrant. Add half of sugar mixture, shaking pecans constantly. When sugar begins to caramelize, add remaining sugar mixture, shaking pecans constantly until well coated. Turn out to cool and separate.

◆◆◆

2 cups nuts or 6 servings. Each serving contains about: 264 calories; I,180 mg sodium; 0 cholesterol; I4 grams fat; 37 grams carbohydrate; 2 grams protein; 2.24 grams fiber.

SOUPS

◆◆◆

For reasons we cannot explain, soups are high on the list of most frequently requested "Culinary SOS" dishes. Maybe it's because so many restaurants produce outstanding ones—just scan this list and you'll see what we mean. The soups are not just the hearty types you'd expect people to particularly enjoy, such as Hamburger Hamlet's Onion Soup Fondue or Rancho Bernardo Inn's Albóndigas Soup. They are light and airy, sometimes creamy yet containing no cream, such as Il Moro's Cream of Zucchini Soup and Luna Park's Asparagus Soup. There are soups for every occasion, whether for a holiday bash (Steak Soup) or a dainty lunch (Cold Cucumber Soup). There are soups to warm you up in a flash (Sweet Potato and White Corn Soup) and soups that cool you off (Gazpacho). There are soups of different ethnic persuasions that might have particular appeal, too. You'll find them all here.

Asparagus Soup ◆ Luna Park

Cream of Black Bean Soup ◆ Baily Wine Country Cafe

Canadian Cheese Soup ◆ Fiddlers Three

Corn Chowder ◆ Chaya Brasserie

Onion Soup Fondue ◆ Hamburger Hamlet

Garlic Soup ◆ Artz Rib House

Toscana Soup ◆ Olive Garden

Sweet Potato and White Corn Soup ◆ Grand Hotel

Butternut Squash Soup ◆ Bistro Garden at Coldwater

Fire-Roasted Tomato Soup ◆ El Torito Grill

Cream of Zucchini Soup ◆ Il Moro

Albóndigas Soup ◆ Rancho Bernardo Inn

Goulash Soup ◆ Cafe Cego

Steak Soup ◆ Clinkerdagger, Bickenstaff & Pitts

Chicken and Lime Soup ◆ El Torito Restaurants

Clam Chowder ◆ Legal Sea Foods

Cold Cucumber Soup ◆ Scandia

Gazpacho ◆ Velvet Turtle

ASPARAGUS SOUP

Luna Park, West Hollywood

There is no cream in this recipe from health-conscious Luna Park. Instead potato is the thickener, and raw spinach is used to enhance color.

SOUP:

1/2 onion, chopped
1 large baking potato, peeled and chopped
1 tablespoon butter or oil
2 1/2 bunches asparagus, cut diagonally in pieces (about 2 1/2 pounds)
Water
1 bunch spinach, washed and stemmed (about 1 pound)
Salt, pepper
1 teaspoon to 1 tablespoon vinegar (optional)
3 tablespoons chopped Italian parsley, for garnish

FRIED ASPARAGUS:

3 asparagus spears
2 tablespoons all-purpose flour
1 egg, beaten
1/4 cup Italian bread crumbs
Oil for frying

SOUP:

Sauté onion and potato in butter in large saucepan over medium heat until onion is soft, 6 to 8 minutes. Add asparagus and sauté until bright green, 3 to 4 minutes. Add enough water to reach 1/2 to 1 inch above asparagus. Bring to boil and simmer 20 minutes.

Transfer asparagus mixture to blender and puree in batches with spinach leaves until smooth.

Strain soup through sieve. Return to saucepan and bring to boil. Reduce heat and simmer 5 to 10 minutes. Add salt, pepper and vinegar to taste. Garnish with Fried Asparagus and parsley.

FRIED ASPARAGUS:

Dredge asparagus in flour, dip in beaten egg and roll in bread crumbs. Heat enough oil to cover asparagus in skillet over medium heat. Add asparagus and fry until golden brown, 1 to 2 minutes. Remove with slotted spatula and drain on paper towel. Cut spears on bias into thirds.

◆◆◆

6 servings. Each serving, with Fried Asparagus, contains about: 361 calories; 210 mg sodium; 62 mg cholesterol; 23 grams fat; 17 grams carbohydrate; 24 grams protein; 1.81 grams fiber.

CREAM of BLACK BEAN SOUP

Baily Wine Country Cafe, Temecula

A nice soup for a wintry night. Try it with a dollop of sour cream and a sprinkle of cilantro.

1 pound dried black beans
1/2 onion, chopped
1 clove garlic, minced
1 tablespoon butter
1 can (8 ounces) peeled and chopped tomatoes
1 Anaheim chile, roasted, peeled and chopped
6 cups chicken broth, plus extra if needed
1/2 bunch cilantro, chopped
2 teaspoons salt
1/2 teaspoon pepper
2 cups half and half or whipping cream
Hot pepper sauce

Cover beans with enough water to cover by 2 inches. Soak at least 8 hours or overnight. Drain.

Sauté onion and garlic in butter in heavy saucepan over medium heat about 3 minutes. Add beans, tomatoes, chile, chicken broth, cilantro, salt and pepper and cook over low heat 1 hour. Add half and half and continue to cook 30 minutes.

Puree in batches in blender. Add more broth if soup is too thick. Stir in hot pepper sauce to taste.

8 servings. Each serving contains about: 323 calories; 1,217 mg sodium; 27 mg cholesterol; 10 grams fat; 41 grams carbohydrate; 18 grams protein; 3.27 grams fiber.

CANADIAN CHEESE SOUP

Fiddlers Three

Fiddlers Three Canadian Cheese Soup is such an old recipe and so frequently requested that we've lost track of its origins. We believe it came from a now closed restaurant in the Sylmar area of the San Fernando Valley.

I cup shredded carrots
I cup thinly sliced celery
2/3 cup thinly sliced onion
2 1/2 tablespoons chicken soup base
2 1/2 cups water
1/3 cup all-purpose flour
3 cups milk
I pound sharp natural Cheddar cheese, shredded
Salt, pepper

Combine carrots, celery, onion, chicken soup base and water in large saucepan. Cover and simmer until vegetables are tender, 10 to 12 minutes.

Blend flour and half of milk and add to vegetable mixture, stirring well. Stir in remaining milk and cook soup until thickened, about 15 minutes. Add cheese and stir just until melted. Season to taste with salt and pepper.

◆◆◆

6 servings. Each serving contains about: 424 calories; 998 mg sodium; 96 mg cholesterol; 30 grams fat; 15 grams carbohydrate; 24 grams protein.

CORN CHOWDER

Chaya Brasserie, West Hollywood

Anyone with cravings for a good corn soup will find this, from one of Hollywood's finest "in" restaurants, extra satisfying.

12 ounces boned chicken breast
1 large onion
1 large leek, white part only
1 large stalk celery
1 large carrot
8 ounces mushrooms
1 clove garlic
1/4 cup (1/2 stick) butter
1/4 cup all-purpose flour
1 can (11 ounces) whole sweet corn kernels
2 quarts chicken broth
1/2 cup milk
1 bay leaf
Salt, pepper
1/4 cup whipping cream

Chop chicken, onion, leek, celery and carrot into large dice. Thinly slice mushrooms and garlic.

Melt butter in large saucepan. Add onion, leek, celery and carrot and sauté over medium heat 10 minutes. Add mushrooms and garlic and cook until mushrooms soften, 6 to 8 minutes. Add chicken and cook until chicken is heated through, about 5 minutes.

Stir in flour until smooth and cook, stirring, 5 minutes. Add 3/4 of the corn. Gradually stir in broth and milk.

In blender, coarsely chop remaining corn at medium speed. Stir chopped corn into soup mixture. Add bay leaf and salt and pepper to taste. Simmer 10 minutes. Discard bay leaf. Stir in cream and heat through.

8 servings. Each serving contains about: 228 calories; 1,021 mg sodium; 46 mg cholesterol; 11 grams fat; 18 grams carbohydrate; 15 grams protein; 0.96 gram fiber.

ONION SOUP FONDUE

Hamburger Hamlet, Los Angeles

From one of the oldest hamburger restaurant chains in the Southland, this French onion soup has been a favorite of our readers for years.

4 large onions, very thinly sliced
Butter
I teaspoon Dijon mustard
Freshly ground pepper
3 quarts beef broth
5 beef bouillon cubes
I cup water
I 1/4 cups dry white wine
12 slices baguette, 1/4 inch thick
1/4 cup applejack
I 1/2 cups freshly grated Parmesan cheese
Monterey Jack cheese

Cook onions in 3/4 cup (I 1/2 sticks) butter until transparent but still slightly crisp. Add mustard and sprinkle with pepper to taste. Combine broth, bouillon cubes, water and wine in large kettle. Add onions and simmer, stirring occasionally, 30 to 45 minutes. Soup may be served at this point.

Otherwise, sauté bread slices in additional butter until golden brown. Place I teaspoon applejack, 2 tablespoons Parmesan cheese and I slice bread in each of 12 large soup bowls. Ladle in soup. Top with 3 or 4 thin slices Monterey Jack cheese. Place bowls on baking sheet and broil until cheese melts and bubbles.

◆◆◆

12 servings. Each serving contains about: 293 calories; 2,340 mg sodium; 45 mg cholesterol; 19 grams fat; 15 grams carbohydrate; 12 grams protein; 0.26 gram fiber.

GARLIC SOUP

Artz Rib House, Austin, Texas

Art Blondin, the owner of Artz Rib House, created this satisfying soup strictly for garlic lovers.

1/2 cup (1 stick) butter
2 heads garlic, cloves peeled and crushed
1 onion, chopped
1/2 cup all-purpose flour
1 teaspoon paprika
1/8 teaspoon cayenne pepper
1 teaspoon white pepper
1/2 teaspoon dried thyme
6 cups chicken broth
1 lemon, 1/2 juiced and 1/2 sliced
2 tablespoons chopped fresh parsley
Croutons

Melt butter in 3-quart saucepan over medium heat. Add garlic and sauté until barely browned, about 3 minutes. Remove with slotted spoon and set aside.

Add onion to pan and sauté until tender, about 3 minutes. Add flour, paprika, cayenne, white pepper and thyme and cook, stirring constantly, 3 minutes.

Add chicken broth and bring to boil over medium-high heat, stirring often. Reduce heat to low. Remove 1/2 cup broth from pan and process in blender with reserved garlic until smooth, 2 to 3 seconds. Return to pan. Add lemon juice and parsley and stir well. Simmer 10 minutes. Serve with croutons and sliced lemon.

◆◆◆

6 servings. Each serving, without croutons, contains about: 231 calories; 937 mg sodium; 42 mg cholesterol; 17 grams fat; 14 grams carbohydrate; 7 grams protein; 0.39 gram fiber.

TOSCANA SOUP

The Olive Garden

Many readers who request this recipe from the Olive Garden, a national restaurant chain, describe the soup as "light and wonderful." It's great with crusty bread and a glass of wine.

8 ounces Italian sausage links
3/4 cup diced onion
1 slice bacon, cut into 1/4-inch dice
1 1/4 teaspoons minced garlic
4 cups nonfat, low-sodium chicken broth
2 baking potatoes, peeled, halved lengthwise and cut into 1/4-inch slices
2 cups kale or other greens, thinly sliced
1/3 cup heavy whipping cream
Salt

Preheat oven to 350 degrees. Place sausages on baking sheet and bake 15 to 20 minutes. Halve lengthwise, then cut diagonally into 1/2-inch slices.

Combine onion and bacon in 3- to 4-quart saucepan and cook over medium heat until onion is almost transparent, 3 to 4 minutes. Add garlic and cook 1 minute.

Add chicken broth and potatoes. Bring to boil, reduce heat and simmer 15 minutes. Add greens, sausage, whipping cream and salt to taste. Simmer 5 minutes longer.

6 servings. Each serving contains about: 295 calories; 373 mg sodium; 43 mg cholesterol; 19 grams fat; 21 grams carbohydrate; 12 grams protein; 0.63 gram fiber.

SWEET POTATO and WHITE CORN SOUP

Grand Hotel, Mackinac Island, Michigan

An unusual, homey soup for the holiday season.

2 tablespoons vegetable oil
1 large white onion, diced
1 cup fresh or frozen white corn kernels
1/3 cup white wine
3 large sweet potatoes, baked, peeled and diced
5 cups chicken broth
1/4 cup mixed finely chopped fresh thyme, basil and tarragon
1 tablespoon finely chopped pickled ginger
Salt, pepper
1 cup half and half
1/4 cup diced cooked celery
1/4 cup diced cooked white potato
1/4 cup cooked fresh or frozen white corn kernels
Chopped chives or croutons

Heat oil in soup pot over medium heat. Add onion and raw corn kernels and sauté 10 minutes. Add wine, sweet potatoes, 4 cups chicken broth, herbs, ginger and salt and pepper to taste. Simmer 10 minutes. Add half and half and simmer 5 minutes longer.

Transfer mixture to blender and puree well. Add up to 1 cup more stock if needed to thin soup. Strain soup. Add cooked celery, potato and corn kernels. Serve in cups or soup bowls and garnish with chopped chives or croutons.

◆◆◆

6 servings. Each serving, without croutons, contains about: 241 calories; 729 mg sodium; 16 mg cholesterol; 11 grams fat; 28 grams carbohydrate; 8 grams protein; 1.09 grams fiber.

BUTTERNUT SQUASH SOUP

The Bistro Garden at Coldwater, Studio City

The Bistro Garden is famous for its wonderfully fresh soups. Here's one.

2 small butternut squash, about 4 pounds
2 onions, sliced
2 tablespoons butter
I leek, white part only, sliced
4 cups chicken broth
I tablespoon sugar
1/2 teaspoon curry powder
1/8 teaspoon ground cumin
Salt
White pepper
1/4 cup hot whipping cream

Preheat oven to 450 degrees. Cut squash in half and scoop out seeds and fibers. Tightly wrap each half in foil. Place on baking sheet and roast until very tender, about I hour. Scoop out flesh with spoon and set aside.

In large saucepan, sauté onions in I tablespoon butter over medium heat until tender. Add leek and squash and cook 5 minutes. Add chicken broth, sugar, curry powder, cumin, salt and white pepper to taste.

Puree soup mixture in blender, a batch at a time, until smooth. Return to pot. Blend last batch with remaining tablespoon butter and cream. Return to remaining soup, stirring, and heat through. Adjust seasoning and thin with a little more chicken broth or cream if necessary.

◆◆◆

8 servings. Each serving contains about: 194 calories; 463 mg sodium; 19 mg cholesterol; 7 grams fat; 31 grams carbohydrate; 6 grams protein; 2.48 grams fiber.

FIRE-ROASTED TOMATO SOUP

El Torito Grill, Beverly Hills

Readers love this soup from El Torito Grill, part of the country's largest Mexican restaurant chain.

SOUP:
3 pounds tomatoes
1 ounce chicken, beef or pork chorizo
1 poblano chile, seeded and chopped
1/2 medium onion, diced
1/4 teaspoon dried oregano
1 large clove garlic, chopped
1 1/2 cups chicken broth
1 cup whipping cream
Salt
White pepper
Cayenne pepper
1 small ear corn, roasted, kernels removed to equal 1/2 cup (see Chef's Tip, page 41)
Cilantro sprigs, for garnish

CREMA FRESCA:
2/3 cup sour cream
1/3 cup half and half

AVOCADO SAUCE:
1 large Haas avocado, peeled and diced
1 tablespoon juice from pickled jalapeño
1 tablespoon minced cilantro
1 green onion, chopped
1 serrano chile, chopped
1 clove garlic, chopped
Salt
Water

SOUP:

Scorch tomatoes over charcoal grill, preferably using mesquite charcoal. Cool slightly.

Sauté chorizo in large saucepan until cooked through. Add chile, onion, oregano and garlic and sauté until onion is transparent. Add unpeeled tomatoes and chicken broth and bring to boil. Simmer 10 to 15 minutes. Add cream, salt, white pepper and cayenne.

Puree soup in batches in blender until smooth. Return to pot. Add corn and heat through. Ladle into heated bowls. Using separate squeeze bottles, drizzle Crema Fresca and Avocado Sauce over soup, or dollop over soup if desired. Garnish with cilantro sprigs.

CREMA FRESCA:

Blend sour cream and half and half in small bowl.

AVOCADO SAUCE:

Combine avocado, jalapeño juice, cilantro, onion, serrano chile, garlic, salt and 1/4 cup water in blender container and blend to form thick liquid, adding more water if necessary.

❖ *Chef's Tip*: To roast corn, preheat oven to 400 degrees. Pull back cornhusk and remove silk; replace husk over ear. Place corn on oven rack and roast 35 minutes. Alternatively, remove husk and silk from corn. Wrap corn in foil and broil 7 inches from heat source 15 to 20 minutes, turning frequently.

◆◆◆

8 servings. Each serving contains about: 265 calories; 269 mg sodium; 57 mg cholesterol; 21 grams fat; 16 grams carbohydrate; 6 grams protein; 1.87 grams fiber.

CREAM of ZUCCHINI SOUP

Il Moro, West Los Angeles

Il Moro shows us how potato is used to achieve the starchy thickness necessary for a well-balanced, velvety soup without cream or butter.

5 tablespoons olive oil
1 large onion, chopped
8 zucchini, chopped
2 boiling potatoes, peeled and chopped
Salt, pepper
2 quarts chicken broth
1 bunch basil, chopped
1 bay leaf
Garlic croutons (optional)

Heat oil in large saucepan over medium heat. Add onion and sauté until softened. Add zucchini, potatoes and salt and pepper to taste and cook several minutes. Stir in chicken broth and cook over medium heat until potatoes are soft, about 30 minutes. Add basil and bay leaf and simmer 10 minutes longer. Remove from heat. Discard bay leaf. Puree soup in blender until smooth and creamy. Serve with garlic croutons, if desired.

◆◆◆

8 servings. Each serving, without croutons, contains about: 130 calories; 430 mg sodium; 0 cholesterol; 9 grams fat; 8 grams carbohydrate; 5 grams protein; 0.73 gram fiber.

ALBÓNDIGAS SOUP

Rancho Bernardo Inn, San Diego

This traditional Mexican soup makes a heartwarming dish on a chilly night.

1 1/2 pounds ground beef
1/2 cup finely chopped onion
3/4 cup finely diced celery
1/4 cup finely diced green bell pepper
1 tablespoon minced garlic
1 teaspoon ground cumin
2 eggs
1/2 cup rice
2 tablespoons dry bread crumbs
Salt, pepper
2 tablespoons olive oil
1/2 cup diced carrot
1 cup chopped tomato
10 cups chicken broth
1 bunch cilantro
Tortillas (optional)

Preheat oven to 350 degrees. Combine beef, onion, 1/4 cup celery, green pepper, garlic, cumin, eggs, rice and bread crumbs. Season to taste with salt and pepper and mix well. Form into 30 small meatballs. Arrange on baking sheet and bake 20 minutes. Set aside.

Heat olive oil in saucepan. Add carrot and remaining 1/2 cup celery and sauté until celery is translucent. Add tomato and chicken broth. Season to taste with salt and pepper. Bring to boil, reduce heat and simmer 30 minutes. Add meatballs. Discard cilantro stems and add leaves to soup. Serve hot, accompanied by tortillas if desired.

6 servings. Each serving, without tortillas, contains about: 446 calories; 1,460 mg sodium; 136 mg cholesterol; 26 grams fat; 22 grams carbohydrate; 28 grams protein; 0.64 gram fiber.

GOULASH SOUP

Cafe Cego, Rolling Hills Estates

Don't be alarmed by the large amounts of paprika called for in this recipe. The spice is derived from sweet and mild varieties of red pepper, far less pungent than cayenne pepper and chili powders.

1/4 cup vegetable oil
4 large onions, diced
2 tablespoons minced garlic
I pound beef top sirloin, diced
1/4 cup Hungarian paprika
1/4 cup Spanish paprika
I can (6 ounces) tomato paste
6 plum tomatoes, peeled and diced
12 cups chicken broth
6 bay leaves
1/2 teaspoon fresh thyme leaves
I pound boiling potatoes, peeled and diced
Salt, pepper

Heat oil in stockpot and sauté onions and garlic until wilted, about 10 minutes. Add meat and sauté over medium-high heat until browned, 10 minutes. Add paprikas and stir with wooden spoon until a few shades lighter and fragrant, about 5 minutes. Add tomato paste and stir over low heat I minute. Add tomatoes, broth, bay leaves and thyme and bring to boil over medium heat. Reduce heat to low and add potatoes. Simmer until potatoes are tender and meat is done, 15 to 20 minutes. Season to taste with salt and pepper.

8 servings. Each serving contains about: 281 calories; 1,246 mg sodium; 27 mg cholesterol; 12 grams fat; 26 grams carbohydrate; 20 grams protein; 2.49 grams fiber.

STEAK SOUP

Clinkerdagger, Bickenstaff & Pitts, Portland, Oregon

This recipe has been popular with our readers since 1982, when Clinker-dagger first shared the recipe, and long after the restaurant changed hands (it's now Hall Street Bar & Grill).

I cup (2 sticks) butter or margarine
I 1/2 cups chopped onions
I 1/2 cups sliced peeled carrots
I cup diced celery
I cup all-purpose flour
I pound ground beef
2 1/2 quarts water
I can (8 ounces) chopped tomatoes
1/3 cup beef stock base
Pepper
I package (10 ounces) frozen mixed vegetables

Melt butter in large saucepan over medium heat. Add onions, carrots and celery and sauté until onions are tender, about 15 minutes. Add flour and stir until well blended and smooth. Cook until mixture boils around edges, but do not overcook or roux will break down. Set aside.

Preheat oven to 350 degrees. Crumble ground beef onto rimmed baking sheet and pat into 1-inch-thick layer. Bake 15 to 20 minutes or until meat is browned (color of beef will determine color of soup).

Drain meat. Break into 1/2-inch chunks. Add half of water to saucepan with cooked vegetables and bring to simmer. Add tomatoes, beef chunks and beef stock base. Season with pepper. Cook and stir 10 minutes. Add remaining water and frozen vegetables. Cook 5 minutes longer or until vegetables are tender; do not boil.

16 servings. Each serving contains about: 287 calories; 1,439 mg sodium; 63 mg cholesterol; 22 grams fat; 16 grams carbohydrate; 8 grams protein; 0.82 gram fiber.

CHICKEN and LIME SOUP

El Torito Restaurants

Hominy, corn or other ingredients can be added as garnishes in this excellent chicken soup.

I quart chicken broth
Juice of 2 limes
I teaspoon dried Mexican oregano
I teaspoon dried basil
I teaspoon pureed chipotle chile
I bay leaf
Salt
White pepper
2 chicken breast halves, cooked, skinned and shredded
I cup julienne-cut tomatoes
1/2 cup julienne-cut red onion
I tablespoon minced cilantro
4 ounces jalapeño Jack cheese, cut into cubes
2 corn tortillas, cut into strips
I avocado, peeled and sliced
4 lime slices
4 cilantro sprigs

Combine broth, lime juice, oregano, basil, pureed chipotle and bay leaf in stock-pot. Season to taste with salt and white pepper. Bring to boil and simmer 15 minutes.

Add shredded chicken, tomatoes, red onion and cilantro and bring to boil. Simmer 5 minutes. Adjust seasonings to taste. Ladle very hot soup into heated soup bowls. Drop in cheese cubes. Top each serving with a few tortilla strips, avocado slices, a lime slice and a cilantro sprig.

4 servings. Each serving contains about: 313 calories; 1,102 mg sodium; 39 mg cholesterol; 20 grams fat; 16 grams carbohydrate; 19 grams protein; 1.5 grams fiber.

CLAM CHOWDER

Legal Sea Foods, Cambridge, Massachusetts

This recipe came with a caveat: "Don't try to economize by cutting back on the amount of clams or cream."

6 pounds littleneck clams
I clove garlic
I cup water
2 ounces salt pork, finely chopped
2 cups chopped onions
3 tablespoons all-purpose flour
3 cups fish stock or bottled clam juice
I 1/2 pounds boiling potatoes, peeled and cut into 1/2-inch cubes
2 cups whipping cream
Oyster crackers (optional)

Scrub clams well under cold running water. Place in large pot with garlic and water. Steam clams just until opened, about 6 to 10 minutes depending on size. Drain and shell clams, reserving broth (there should be about 4 cups).

Mince clam flesh and set aside. Strain clam broth through cheesecloth and set aside.

In large soup pot, fry salt pork over medium heat until crisp. Remove cracklings and set aside. Add onions and sauté in pork fat over medium heat, stirring frequently, until cooked through but not browned, about 6 minutes. Stir in flour and cook, stirring, 3 minutes. Add reserved clam broth and fish stock and whisk to remove any flour lumps.

Bring liquid to boil. Add potatoes, then reduce heat and simmer until potatoes are tender, about 15 minutes. Stir in reserved clams, salt pork cracklings and cream; heat through. Serve in large soup bowls with oyster crackers, if desired.

8 servings. Each serving contains about: 401 calories; 475 mg sodium; 116 mg cholesterol; 26 grams fat; 25 grams carbohydrate; 16 grams protein; 0.61 gram fiber.

COLD CUCUMBER SOUP

Scandia, West Hollywood

It's hard to beat a tried-and-true summery soup like this longtime favorite.

3 medium cucumbers
2 tablespoons butter
I leek, chopped
2 bay leaves
I tablespoon all-purpose flour
3 cups chicken broth
I teaspoon salt
I cup half and half
Juice of 1/2 lemon
Chopped fresh dill
Sour cream

Peel and thinly slice 2 cucumbers. Melt butter in skillet over medium-low heat. Add sliced cucumbers, leek and bay leaves and cook slowly until vegetables are tender but not brown. Discard bay leaves.

Stir in flour. Add chicken broth and salt and bring to boil, then reduce heat and simmer 20 to 30 minutes, stirring occasionally. Puree soup through sieve or in blender and chill several hours.

Peel, halve and seed remaining cucumber, then grate. Add to soup with half and half, lemon juice and chopped dill to taste. Serve in chilled soup cups and top each serving with a dollop of sour cream.

◆◆◆

6 servings. Each serving contains about: 155 calories; 1,240 mg sodium; 26 mg cholesterol; 10 grams fat; 9 grams carbohydrate; 8 grams protein; 1.12 grams fiber.

GAZPACHO
Velvet Turtle, Los Angeles

The now-closed Velvet Turtle chain left us with its outstanding California-style gazpacho soup, a reader favorite for many years.

1 can (46 ounces) tomato juice
1 green bell pepper, seeded and minced
1 onion, minced
1 cucumber, peeled and minced
2 small canned green chiles, minced
1 tablespoon Worcestershire sauce
1 teaspoon Mexican seasoning blend
1/2 teaspoon minced garlic
1 tablespoon olive oil
1 tablespoon chopped chives
2 drops hot pepper sauce
Salt
White pepper
Lemon wedges

Combine tomato juice, bell pepper, onion, cucumber, chiles, Worcestershire sauce, Mexican seasoning, garlic, olive oil, chives and hot pepper sauce. Season to taste with salt and white pepper. Chill thoroughly. Serve with lemon wedges.

◆◆◆

8 servings. Each serving contains about: 58 calories; 661 mg sodium; 0 mg cholesterol; 2 grams fat; 10 grams carbohydrates; 2 grams protein; 1.48 grams fiber.

BREADS

◆◆◆

California restaurants have long been a mecca for novelty breads, yet readers of the "Culinary SOS" column apparently target only certain types, if our requests are any indication. Cornbread is a top favorite. Say "pancakes" and millions of hands will go up.

One reason may be that while readers enjoy eating a wide range of novelty breads, they seem to request only those that can be conveniently prepared at home. Gone are the days of kneading and coaxing the dough to rise for hours on end. Besides, restaurants and, particularly, bakeries are not inclined to part with recipes they consider proprietary. Commercial recipes are often so large and complex, with stabilizers and modifiers, that conversion to home-size formulas would be nearly impossible. Once the chemical balance is disrupted, texture, taste and overall results are dramatically altered.

There is surprising variety within the categories. For instance, we've gotten requests for dozens of pancake recipes, including the buckwheat, lemon and German pancakes given here. Among cornbreads, there are crumbly New York-style muffins as well as and Meini, the flattish Italian corn cakes from Il Fornaio. Such international links are on the rise, and so are recipes from around the country. In fact, increased travel in the last 30 years has prompted many reader requests for breads from restaurants as far afield as Hawaii and Louisiana.

Pumpernickel Toast ✦ Perino's

Garlic Cheese Bread ✦ Stuart Anderson's Black Angus Restaurants

Focaccia ✦ The White House Restaurant

Scones ✦ Ritz-Carlton Huntington Hotel

Bran Muffins ✦ Stardust Hotel Resort and Casino

Al's New York Corn Muffins ✦ Al's Diner

Sweet Cornmeal Buns (Meini) ✦ Il Fornaio

Buckwheat Cakes ✦ Wigwam Motel

Zucchini-Nut Muffins ✦ Clifton's Cafeteria

Sourdough French Toast ✦ Marston's

Lemon Cloud Pancakes ✦ Pluto's

German Apple Pancakes ✦ The Bistro Garden at Coldwater

PUMPERNICKEL TOAST

Perino's, Hancock Park

Perino's pumpernickel toast strips were usually brought to the table tucked in crisp white napkins as a nibble before the orders were taken. The restaurant is closed, but many Los Angeles restaurants have adopted the famous toast.

I loaf unsliced pumpernickel, frozen
1/2 cup (I stick) butter
I to 2 cloves garlic, crushed
1/2 cup freshly grated Parmesan cheese

Slice bread paper-thin with sharp knife. Melt butter over low heat. Add garlic and cheese and stir briefly to blend well. Using pastry brush, spread one side of each bread slice with butter mixture.

Preheat oven to 275 degrees. Arrange bread slices in single layer on ungreased baking sheets. Bake until crisp, about 15 to 20 minutes. (Bread will curl slightly at edges.)

Cool, then store in airtight container until ready to use. Serve as appetizer or with soups and salads.

◆◆◆

30 to 40 slices. Each of 30 slices contains about: 72 calories; 147 mg sodium; 10 mg cholesterol; 4 grams fat; 8 grams carbohydrate; 2 grams protein; 0.17 gram fiber.

GARLIC-CHEESE BREAD

Stuart Anderson's Black Angus Restaurants

This bread is wonderful served with chili or pasta, or cut into small pieces as an appetizer.

1 loaf French bread
1/2 cup (1 stick) butter, softened
1 cup shredded Asiago cheese
1 cup shredded Monterey Jack cheese
1 cup mayonnaise
1 bunch green onions, chopped
2 cloves garlic, pureed

   Split French bread loaf in half lengthwise. In bowl combine butter, Asiago, Monterey Jack, mayonnaise, green onions and garlic and blend well. Spread cut side of bread with mixture.
   Preheat oven to 350 degrees. Bake bread 7 minutes, then place under broiler about 3 minutes longer. Cut into slices and serve.

◆◆◆

10 servings. Each serving contains about: 329 calories; 637 mg sodium; 46 mg cholesterol; 23 grams fat; 22 grams carbohydrate; 9 grams protein; 0.11 gram fiber.

FOCACCIA
The White House Restaurant, Laguna Beach

Focaccia is served as you wait for your meal at the White House Restaurant.

1 bunch parsley, leaves only
1 bunch rosemary, leaves only
1 bunch sage, leaves only
4 cloves garlic
1/3 cup olive oil
Salt
9 cups all-purpose flour
1 tablespoon sugar
1 teaspoon dried oregano
1 teaspoon dried basil
1/3 cup freshly grated Parmesan cheese
1 envelope dry yeast
4 1/2 cups warm water

Puree parsley, rosemary, sage, garlic, olive oil and 1/4 teaspoon salt in blender until mixture resembles pesto.

Combine 1 tablespoon salt, flour, sugar, oregano, basil, Parmesan cheese and 3 tablespoons herb pesto in mixing bowl and blend at low speed using dough hook attachment.

Dissolve yeast in warm water and pour slowly into mixing bowl. Mix at low speed until dough is soft, smooth and sticky. Cover dough with damp cloth and let rise in warm place until doubled in bulk, about 1 hour.

Transfer dough to greased 17 x 13-inch rimmed baking sheet. Using wet hands, pat and smooth into corners of baking sheet.

Rub top of dough with remaining pesto mixture. Make indentations throughout dough with fingertips. Cover and let rise until doubled in bulk, about 45 minutes.

Preheat oven to 350 degrees. Bake focaccia until golden brown, about 45 minutes, rotating once halfway through cooking. Turn out onto rack to cool. Cut into squares.

◆◆◆

16 to 24 squares. Each of 24 squares contains about: 195 calories; 347 mg sodium; 1 mg cholesterol; 4 grams fat; 34 grams carbohydrate; 5 grams protein; 0.25 gram fiber.

SCONES

Ritz-Carlton Huntington Hotel, Pasadena

Handle the dough as little as possible for light and fluffy scones. Overmixing tends to toughen biscuit-like products and make them heavy.

1/4 cup (1/2 stick) butter, softened
1 cup powdered sugar
4 cups pastry flour
1 1/4 tablespoons baking powder
1 egg
1 1/4 cups milk
Pinch of salt
4 ounces dried apricots, chopped
4 ounces raisins

Cream butter and powdered sugar. Add pastry flour, baking powder, egg, milk and salt, mixing just to blend; do not overmix. Add apricots and raisins.

Preheat oven to 400 degrees. Using ice cream scoop, scoop out dough and drop onto baking sheet. Press each scoop of dough into 4-inch round. Bake scones until lightly golden, 8 to 10 minutes.

◆◆◆

15 scones. Each scone contains about: 222 calories; 235 mg sodium; 25 mg cholesterol; 4 grams fat; 43 grams carbohydrate; 4 grams protein; 0.33 gram fiber.

BRAN MUFFINS

Stardust Hotel Resort and Casino, Las Vegas

If you prefer moist muffins, add crushed pineapple to the batter. If you use canned pineapple, drain it first.

1 1/4 cups packed dark or light brown sugar
2 tablespoons honey
1/4 cup vegetable oil, plus extra for greasing muffin cups
2 eggs
1 cup buttermilk
2 cups all-purpose flour
2 cups bran cereal
1 teaspoon baking powder
Pinch of salt
1/2 cup raisins
1/4 cup crushed pineapple (optional)

Beat brown sugar, honey, oil, eggs and buttermilk in large bowl until smooth. Stir in flour, bran, baking powder and salt. Fold in raisins and pineapple.

Preheat oven to 375 degrees. Grease 12 muffin cups. Divide batter among prepared cups and bake until toothpick inserted in center comes out clean, about 20 minutes. Let cool 10 minutes, then remove muffins from pan. Serve warm.

◆◆◆

12 muffins. Each muffin, without pineapple, contains about: 257 calories; 93 mg sodium; 36 mg cholesterol; 7 grams fat; 49 grams carbohydrate; 7 grams protein; 0.48 gram fiber.

AL'S NEW YORK CORN MUFFINS

Al's Diner, New York City

The recipe for these New York-style corn muffins is my father's. He baked them every day for the breakfast crowd at Al's Diner, his little cafe in Greenwich Village during the mid-1940s.

2 cups cornmeal
1 cup all-purpose flour
1 cup sugar
1 tablespoon baking powder
1/4 teaspoon salt
1 cup shortening, plus more for greasing pan
1 egg
1 1/4 cups milk
1 teaspoon vanilla extract

Combine cornmeal, flour, sugar, baking powder and salt in large bowl. Cut in shortening until mixture resembles coarse crumbs. Beat egg in small bowl. Stir in milk and vanilla. Add to cornmeal mixture, stirring just to moisten; do not overmix.

Preheat oven to 350 degrees. Grease 12 muffin cups. Fill each cup 2/3 full with batter. Bake muffins until golden, 20 to 25 minutes.

Let muffins cool thoroughly in cups before loosening from pan or they will fall apart. Carefully remove from pan.

12 muffins. Each muffin contains about: 354 calories; 175 mg sodium; 20 mg cholesterol; 18 grams fat; 43 grams carbohydrate; 4 grams protein; 0.17 gram fiber.

SWEET CORNMEAL BUNS (Meini)

Il Fornaio, Los Angeles

These disk-shaped Italian cornmeal buns are excellent with salads and soups.

1 1/2 cups unbleached all-purpose flour
2 teaspoons baking powder
1 cup fine yellow cornmeal
3/4 cup (1 1/2 sticks) unsalted butter, softened
Granulated sugar
2 tablespoons honey
2 egg yolks
1/4 cup whipping cream
1/4 cup milk
1 1/2 teaspoons grated lemon zest
1/2 teaspoon vanilla extract
Powdered sugar

Sift flour, baking powder and cornmeal into bowl. Set aside.

Cream butter with 1/2 cup granulated sugar and honey in large bowl until light and fluffy, about 5 minutes. Add egg yolks one at time, beating well after each addition and scraping down sides of bowl with rubber spatula.

Add half of flour mixture, beating at medium speed until dry ingredients are thoroughly incorporated. Beat in cream, milk, lemon zest and vanilla. Add remaining flour mixture and mix until soft dough forms, about 2 minutes. Dough will be sticky.

Dust hands lightly with flour and divide dough into 12 equal portions, about 3 tablespoons each. Shape each into golf ball–size sphere. With palm of hand, flatten each ball slightly on floured surface into 3/4-inch disk.

Preheat oven to 375 degrees. Butter baking sheet or line with parchment paper. Brush tops of buns lightly with water and sprinkle with granulated sugar.

Bake buns until golden, about 15 to 18 minutes. Let cool completely on baking sheet. Sift powdered sugar over tops. Store in covered container at room temperature up to 5 days.

12 buns. Each bun contains about: 274 calories; 79 mg sodium; 84 mg cholesterol; 15 grams fat; 33 grams carbohydrate; 3 grams protein; 0.11 gram fiber.

BUCKWHEAT CAKES

Wigwam Motel, Holbrook, Arizona

Serve these tasty pancakes with fresh fruit to offset the dark buckwheat color.

3 eggs
2 tablespoons sugar
I teaspoon salt
2 1/2 cups milk
2 cups cake flour
2 cups buckwheat flour
2 tablespoons baking powder
1/4 cup (1/2 stick) butter, melted

Blend eggs, sugar and salt in bowl. Stir in milk. Sift flours and baking powder into large bowl. Whisk in egg mixture. Add melted butter and mix just until incorporated; do not overmix. Let stand 15 to 20 minutes. Batter will be thick.

Drop batter by scant 1/4 cupfuls onto lightly greased griddle and cook until underside is lightly browned and top is starting to bubble. Turn and cook other side until browned and dry.

◆◆◆

8 servings. Each serving contains about: 330 calories; 738 mg sodium; 101 mg cholesterol; 10 grams fat; 50 grams carbohydrate; 11 grams protein; 0.6 gram fiber.

ZUCCHINI-NUT MUFFINS

Clifton's Cafeteria, Los Angeles

We've rated these healthful muffins from Clifton's Cafeteria a solid "10."

3 cups all-purpose flour, sifted
I teaspoon baking powder
I teaspoon baking soda
I teaspoon salt
I teaspoon cinnamon
2 cups sugar
4 eggs
I cup vegetable oil
2 cups coarsely grated unpeeled zucchini
1/2 teaspoon vanilla extract
I cup walnuts, chopped
1/2 cup raisins

Sift together flour, baking powder, baking soda, salt and cinnamon. Set aside.

Combine sugar and eggs in large bowl of electric mixer and beat at medium speed 2 minutes. Add oil in slow, steady stream, beating constantly 2 to 3 minutes. Add zucchini and vanilla and blend well. Stir in walnuts and raisins. Fold in dry ingredients just until batter is evenly moistened; do not overmix.

Preheat oven to 350 degrees. Line 22 muffin cups with paper liners. Fill cups 2/3 full with batter. Bake 25 minutes or until lightly browned. Let cool 10 minutes, then remove muffins from pans.

◆◆◆

22 muffins. Each muffin contains about: 282 calories; 140 mg sodium; 39 mg cholesterol; 15 grams fat; 36 grams carbohydrate; 4 grams protein; 0.41 gram fiber.

SOURDOUGH FRENCH TOAST

Marston's, Pasadena

Owners Sally and Otis Marston claim the French toast at Marston's is the most-ordered item on the breakfast menu. However, they caution, "the sourdough bread has to be truly sour to make it just right."

6 eggs
I teaspoon vanilla extract
4 cups cornflakes
2 teaspoons cinnamon
8 thick slices sourdough bread
Butter
Powdered sugar
Maple syrup

Lightly beat eggs in bowl. Stir in vanilla. Crush cornflakes in shallow pan. Toss with cinnamon.

Halve sourdough bread slices. Dip each half in egg mixture, coating generously. Roll in cornflakes. Cook on well-buttered griddle or heavy skillet over medium heat until golden brown on both sides. Sprinkle with powdered sugar. Serve with maple syrup.

◆◆◆

8 servings. Each serving contains about: 309 calories; 518 mg sodium; 224 mg cholesterol; 10 grams fat; 41 grams carbohydrate; 12 grams protein; 0.15 gram fiber.

LEMON CLOUD PANCAKES

Pluto's, San Francisco

Readers who have tried these pancakes say they are "like biting into clouds." Egg whites and ricotta cheese in the batter virtually act like an air pump.

11 eggs, separated
1 1/4 cups all-purpose flour
1 container (15 ounces) ricotta cheese
Grated zest of 2 lemons
1/3 cup butter, melted
1/3 cup sugar
1 teaspoon salt

Whip egg whites at high speed until stiff peaks form, 3 to 4 minutes.

Beat egg yolks in large bowl. Add flour, ricotta, lemon zest, butter, sugar and salt and mix until batter is smooth. Fold in 1/4 of egg whites to lighten batter, then fold in remaining whites; do not overmix.

Lightly coat griddle with nonstick cooking spray. Heat over medium-low heat. Ladle 1/2 cup batter onto griddle for each pancake. Cook pancakes until light brown, about 4 minutes, then turn and cook 3 minutes more. Serve with a favorite topping.

◆◆◆

24 pancakes. Each pancake contains about: 120 calories; 168 mg sodium; 113 mg cholesterol; 7 grams fat; 8 grams carbohydrate; 6 grams protein; 0.02 gram fiber.

GERMAN APPLE PANCAKES

The Bistro Garden at Coldwater, Studio City

This recipe makes seven man-size pancakes, or enough smaller ones for a crowd.

PANCAKES:

6 eggs
1/2 cup plus 2 tablespoons sugar
I tablespoon vanilla extract
2 1/4 cups milk
4 cups all-purpose flour
7 Granny Smith or Pippin apples, peeled and cored
7 tablespoons butter
Sour cream and jam or marmalade (optional)

CINNAMON SUGAR:

I cup sugar
I tablespoon cinnamon

PANCAKES:

Combine 3 whole eggs, 3 egg yolks, sugar, vanilla and milk in bowl and blend well. Mix in flour. Let stand 15 minutes. Whip 3 remaining egg whites until stiff and fold into batter.

Cut I apple into 1/2-inch slices and sauté in I tablespoon butter in 10-inch stainless steel skillet until lightly browned on both sides. Add I cup batter, cover and cook until golden brown on bottom. Flip over and heat pancake quickly until set. Sprinkle top with Cinnamon Sugar. Place under broiler to brown.

Slide pancake onto serving plate. Sprinkle with additional Cinnamon Sugar if desired. Repeat process with remaining apples, butter and batter, cooking each pancake separately. Serve with sour cream and/or jam or marmalade.

CINNAMON SUGAR:

Mix sugar with cinnamon. Makes about I cup.

7 large pancakes. Each pancake contains about: 702 calories; 415 mg sodium; 32 mg cholesterol; 12 grams fat; 122 grams carbohydrate; 31 grams protein; 0.79 gram fiber.

SALADS

◆◆◆

L os Angeles has probably done more than any other city to promote the salad trend throughout the country. After all, salads have long been associated with glamorous Hollywood stars, who pick at them to stay svelte and healthy.

After taking root here, salad bars mushroomed everywhere. Exotic greens such as arugula and mesclun, once a California obsession, made their way across America.

Northern California vegetable farms became experimental stations for all sorts of greens, baby vegetables and unusual mushrooms. Soon restaurateurs themselves encouraged local farmers to grow exotic plants and herbs to their specifications.

Salads lend themselves to vast improvisation, as you will see from a glance at this chapter. Chicken salad is king, and it comes in many variations. Also popular are such ethnic specialties as Shredded Tofu Salad and Tabbouleh. And new ideas, such as Southwestern Caesar Salad from the El Torito chain, are always popping up.

In this chapter you'll find a salad to suit your every need, from light first course to full-fledged meal in a dish.

Lyonnaise Salad ◆ Mimosa

Pantry Coleslaw ◆ The Original Pantry

Coleslaw without Mayonnaise ◆ Tam O'Shanter

Maude Salad ◆ Chasen's

Leon Salad ◆ La Scala

Southwestern Caesar Salad ◆ El Torito Restaurants

Egg-Free Caesar Salad ◆ Cafe Figaro

Shredded Tofu Salad ◆ Mandarin Deli

Tabbouleh ◆ L.A. Nicola

Brown Rice and Lentil Salad ◆ Courtney's

Black Bean Salad ◆ Lawry's California Center

Chinese Chicken Salad ◆ New Moon Restaurant

Barbecue Chicken Salad ◆ Panda Inn Restaurants

Spinach Chicken Salad ◆ Marmalade Cafe

Chicken Salad with Orange Soufflé ◆ Neiman Marcus

No-Mayo Roasted Chicken Salad ◆ Koo Koo Roo

LYONNAISE SALAD

Mimosa, West Hollywood

Mimosa owner Silvio di Mori was happy to share this classic French recipe, which he says has had a fantastic comeback since eggs are "in" again.

VINAIGRETTE:
1 egg yolk or equivalent pasteurized egg product
1 tablespoon Dijon mustard
Salt, pepper
3 tablespoons red wine vinegar
1/4 cup olive oil or peanut oil

SALAD:
6 eggs
6 ounces smoked bacon, diced
1 tablespoon peanut oil
2 tablespoons red wine vinegar
1/2 cup garlic croutons
12 ounces curly endive (frisée), about 1 head

VINAIGRETTE:
Combine egg yolk, mustard, salt and pepper to taste and vinegar in mixing bowl. Slowly whisk in olive oil. Add small amount of water if dressing is too thick.

SALAD:
Poach eggs in simmering water in shallow skillet, or crack each egg into cup and slowly pour steaming water over. Remove eggs with slotted spoon when whites have cooked and yolks are still soft. Place in ice water and set aside. Reserve cooking water.

Sauté bacon in peanut oil in separate skillet until crisp. Drain off excess fat. While pan is hot, add vinegar, being careful to avoid spatters.

Combine bacon and vinegar in bowl with croutons and curly endive. Toss with Vinaigrette.

Arrange salad on 6 plates. Reheat reserved water. Add eggs and heat 30 seconds. Remove eggs with slotted spoon and place 1 egg on top of each salad. Serve warm.

6 servings. Each serving contains about: 325 calories; 356 mg sodium; 274 mg cholesterol; 30 grams fat; 4 grams carbohydrate; 10 grams protein; 0.51 gram fiber.

PANTRY COLESLAW

The Original Pantry, Los Angeles

One of the oldest restaurants in Los Angeles is famous for its coleslaw, among other items. However, don't expect a perfect reproduction. Recipes broken down from large quantities often lose something in the translation.

3/4 cup mayonnaise
3 tablespoons sugar
1 1/2 tablespoons white wine vinegar
1/3 cup vegetable oil
1/8 teaspoon garlic powder
1/8 teaspoon onion powder
1/8 teaspoon dry mustard
1/8 teaspoon celery salt
Pinch of black pepper
1 tablespoon lemon juice
1/2 cup half and half
1/4 teaspoon salt
1 large head cabbage, very finely shredded

Blend mayonnaise, sugar, vinegar and oil. Add garlic and onion powders, mustard, celery salt, pepper, lemon juice, half and half and salt and stir until smooth. Pour over cabbage in large bowl and toss until well coated.

◆◆◆

8 servings. Each serving contains about: 187 calories; 118 mg sodium; 7 mg cholesterol; 13 grams fat; 17 grams carbohydrate; 2 grams protein; 0.94 gram fiber.

COLESLAW without MAYONNAISE

Tam O'Shanter Inn, Los Angeles

This coleslaw with peanuts and no mayonnaise, enjoyed by countless readers, is served with sandwiches at the Tam.

4 cups shredded cabbage
1/2 cup chopped green onions, including tops
1 cup chopped celery, including leaves
1/4 cup chopped salted peanuts
1/2 teaspoon seasoned salt
1/4 teaspoon seasoned pepper
1/3 cup Italian salad dressing

Lightly toss together cabbage, green onions, celery and peanuts in salad bowl. Sprinkle with seasoned salt and pepper to taste. Pour salad dressing over and toss to coat. Chill thoroughly.

◆◆◆

4 servings. Each serving, with dressing, contains about: 169 calories; 276 mg sodium; 0 cholesterol; 14 grams fat; 10 grams carbohydrate; 4 grams protein; 1.41 grams fiber.

MAUDE SALAD

Chasen's, Beverly Hills

When Chasen's closed, owner Maude Chasen sent us this recipe, which was named after her. The salad comes with a creamy Roquefort dressing.

SALAD:
8 cups shredded mixed iceberg lettuce, romaine and chicory
4 cups diced tomatoes
4 hard-boiled eggs, chopped
2 bunches chopped chives
I cup crumbled Roquefort cheese

CREAMY ROQUEFORT DRESSING:
I cup mayonnaise
3/4 cup sour cream
I to 2 cloves garlic, minced
1/2 cup chili sauce
1/4 cup red wine vinegar
3/4 cup crumbled Roquefort cheese
Salt, pepper

SALAD:
Combine mixed lettuces, tomatoes, eggs and chives in bowl and toss. Chill.
When ready to serve, add Creamy Roquefort Dressing and toss well. Sprinkle top of salad with crumbled Roquefort cheese.

CREAMY ROQUEFORT DRESSING:
Whisk mayonnaise, sour cream, garlic, chili sauce and vinegar in bowl. Stir in Roquefort cheese. Season with salt and pepper to taste. Mix well. Makes about 3 cups.

8 servings. Each serving contains about: 339 calories; 939 mg sodium; 145 mg cholesterol; 25 grams fat; 19 grams carbohydrate; 13 grams protein; 1.05 grams fiber.

LEON SALAD

La Scala, Beverly Hills

La Scala's Leon chopped salad is just as popular today as it was in the 1960s, when it became a fad among celebrities, who could be seen munching on the salad at all hours of the day and night.

SALAD:

I head iceberg lettuce, finely chopped
I head romaine, finely chopped
4 ounces Italian salami, julienned
4 ounces mozzarella cheese, shredded
I can (15 1/2 ounces) garbanzo beans, drained

LEON DRESSING:

1/4 cup vegetable oil
2 tablespoons wine vinegar
I teaspoon dry mustard
1/2 teaspoon salt
1/2 teaspoon black pepper
1/4 cup freshly grated Parmesan cheese

SALAD:

Combine lettuces, salami, cheese and beans in salad bowl. Toss with Leon Dressing.

LEON DRESSING:

Combine oil, vinegar, mustard, salt, pepper and Parmesan and whisk to blend well. Makes about 1/2 cup.

6 servings. Each serving contains about: 327 calories; 994 mg sodium; 33 mg cholesterol; 22 grams fat; 19 grams carbohydrate; 14 grams protein; 3.62 grams fiber.

SOUTHWESTERN CAESAR SALAD
El Torito Restaurants

You will find this version of Caesar salad fascinating. It contains Mexican ingredients such as pepitas (pumpkin seeds) and cotija cheese, which are available in Mexican markets and many supermarkets.

SALAD:
2 corn tortillas
Vegetable oil for deep frying
1 large head romaine
$1/2$ cup grated cotija cheese
Roasted, peeled red pepper strips from a jar or 1 red bell pepper,
   roasted, peeled, seeded and cut into julienne strips
$1/2$ cup roasted pumpkin seeds (pepitas)

CILANTRO-PEPITA DRESSING:
1 medium Anaheim chile, roasted, peeled and seeded
3 tablespoons roasted pumpkin seeds (pepitas)
1 large clove garlic
$1/2$ teaspoon salt
$1/8$ teaspoon freshly ground black pepper
$3/4$ cup vegetable oil
2 tablespoons red wine vinegar
3 tablespoons grated cotija or other hard grating cheese, such as Parmesan
1 small bunch cilantro, stemmed
$3/4$ cup mayonnaise
2 tablespoons water

SALAD:
   Cut tortillas into matchstick-size strips. Heat oil for deep frying and add tortilla strips. Cook a few seconds until crisp. Remove with slotted spoon, drain and set aside.

   Tear romaine into bite-size pieces and divide among six salad plates. Ladle Cilantro-Pepita Dressing on each salad. Sprinkle each dish with cotija cheese and tortilla strips. Arrange four red pepper strips like spokes on top of each salad and garnish with pepitas.

CILANTRO-PEPITA DRESSING:

Combine chile, pepitas, garlic, salt, pepper, oil, vinegar and cheese in blender or food processor and blend about 10 seconds. Gradually blend in cilantro.

Combine mayonnaise and water in large stainless steel bowl and whisk until smooth. Add blended cilantro mixture and mix thoroughly. Transfer to airtight container and refrigerate. Dressing may be stored up to three days. Makes about 2 cups.

◆◆◆

6 servings. Each serving, with dressing, contains about: 407 calories; 489 mg sodium; 13 mg cholesterol; 37 grams fat; 15 grams carbohydrate; 6 grams protein; 3.14 grams fiber.

EGG-FREE CAESAR SALAD

Cafe Figaro, Hollywood

Cafe Figaro, which flourished on Melrose Avenue from the 1970s until the 1990s, kept its menus in tune with the health consciousness of the day.

SALAD:
Inner leaves of 2 heads romaine, cut up
2 tablespoons freshly grated Parmesan cheese

CAESAR DRESSING:
1/4 cup lemon juice
1/2 cup freshly grated Parmesan cheese
2 to 3 whole canned anchovy fillets
2 teaspoons Worcestershire sauce
I teaspoon red wine vinegar
I tablespoon plus I teaspoon Dijon mustard
2 tablespoons pureed garlic
Salt, pepper
3/4 cup olive oil

GARLIC CROUTONS:
6 slices wholewheat bread, crusts trimmed, cubed
3 to 4 tablespoons butter, melted
2 teaspoons garlic powder

SALAD:
   Place romaine leaves in bowl. Add Caesar Dressing and Garlic Croutons. Toss lightly but thoroughly. Sprinkle with Parmesan cheese.

CAESAR DRESSING:
   In blender combine lemon juice, Parmesan, anchovies, Worcestershire sauce, vinegar, mustard, garlic and salt and pepper to taste and blend at medium speed. Add olive oil in stream until dressing is completely blended and smooth. If too thick, thin with up to 1/4 cup cold water. Makes about I 1/2 cups.

GARLIC CROUTONS:

Preheat oven to 425 degrees. Combine bread cubes, butter and garlic powder in bowl and toss to coat well. Spread cubes on baking sheet and bake until golden brown, 8 to 10 minutes. Turn croutons and bake until evenly browned, about 5 more minutes. Let cool.

◆◆◆

6 servings. Each serving, with dressing and croutons, contains about: 432 calories; 622 mg sodium; 25 mg cholesterol; 37 grams fat; 19 grams carbohydrate; 9 grams protein; 1.01 grams fiber.

SHREDDED TOFU SALAD

Mandarin Deli, Los Angeles

Tofu that looks like spaghetti? The tofu strips come in a package, and you cook them in boiling water as you would pasta.

TOFU SALAD:
3 packages (6 ounces each) pressed tofu strips
1 large carrot, shredded
3 pickling cucumbers, shredded
1/2 cup chopped cilantro

GARLIC-SESAME DRESSING:
6 tablespoons minced garlic
6 tablespoons sugar
3/4 teaspoon salt
1/2 cup rice vinegar
1/2 cup Asian sesame oil

TOFU SALAD:

Drop tofu strips into boiling water to cover and boil until soft, 5 to 8 minutes. Drain and rinse in cold water until water runs clear. Drain in strainer 5 minutes.

Combine tofu, carrot, cucumbers and cilantro in salad bowl. Pour Garlic-Sesame Dressing over and toss to mix well. Serve in bowl.

GARLIC-SESAME DRESSING:

Combine garlic, sugar, salt, vinegar and sesame oil and mix well. Makes about 1 1/3 cups.

6 servings. Each serving, with dressing, contains about: 359 calories; 316 mg sodium; 0 cholesterol; 26 grams fat; 23 grams carbohydrate; 14 grams protein; 0.72 gram fiber.

TABBOULEH

L.A. Nicola, Los Angeles

You can turn this salad into a main dish by adding cubes of cooked chicken, turkey or even shrimp.

1/4 cup bulgur wheat
1 1/2 cups finely chopped fresh parsley
4 green onions, chopped
1 large tomato, chopped
6 sprigs mint, chopped
Juice of 2 lemons
1/4 cup vegetable oil
Salt
1 lime, cut into wedges

Cover bulgur generously with cold water and let stand 30 minutes. Drain well.

Combine parsley, onions, tomato, mint and bulgur with hands or two forks. Add lemon juice and oil and season to taste with salt. Mix well. Garnish with lime wedges.

◆◆◆

4 servings. Each serving contains about: 171 calories; 92 mg sodium; 0 cholesterol; 14 grams fat; 11 grams carbohydrate; 2 grams protein; 2.76 grams fiber.

BROWN RICE and LENTIL SALAD

Courtney's, Santa Monica

A great idea for a buffet party. Double or triple the recipe for a crowd.

SALAD:

1 cup long-grain brown rice
1 cup lentils
1/2 cup thinly sliced green onions or red onion
1 cup chopped celery
1 tablespoon chopped fresh parsley
Lettuce (optional)

TARRAGON DRESSING:

6 tablespoons rice vinegar
2 teaspoons honey
2 to 3 tablespoons chopped fresh tarragon or 1 1/2 tablespoons dried
2 cloves garlic, peeled
Salt, pepper
1 cup vegetable oil

SALAD:

Cook rice according to package directions. Rinse in cold water and drain.

Rinse lentils until water runs clear. Drain well. Cook in 4 cups boiling water until tender, about 15 to 20 minutes. Drain. Combine with rice in bowl.

Add onions, celery and parsley to rice mixture. Toss with 1 cup Tarragon Dressing. Refrigerate until ready to serve. Adjust seasonings to taste.

Serve salad on bed of lettuce, if desired, with remaining dressing on the side. Serve chilled or at room temperature.

TARRAGON DRESSING:

Combine vinegar, honey, tarragon and garlic in blender and blend until pureed. Season to taste with salt and pepper. Add oil in thin stream and continue to blend until completely emulsified. Makes about 1 1/3 cups.

6 servings. Each serving, with dressing, contains about: 551 calories; 75 mg sodium; 0 cholesterol; 38 grams fat; 45 grams carbohydrate; 12 grams protein; 2.22 grams fiber.

BLACK BEAN SALAD

Lawry's California Center, Los Angeles

Here's a recipe from the now-closed Lawry's California Center that would make a great side dish for a New Year's buffet.

I pound dried black beans
10 slices bacon, julienned
I medium-size red bell pepper, seeded and chopped
I medium-size green bell pepper, seeded and chopped
I medium-size yellow bell pepper, seeded and chopped
I medium onion, chopped
2 cloves garlic, minced
2 sprigs cilantro, minced
I tablespoon ground cumin
I teaspoon cayenne pepper
2 quarts chicken broth
Salt, pepper
I cup Lawry's Italian dressing

The day before preparing salad, cover black beans generously with cold water and refrigerate overnight.

Drain beans and rinse thoroughly in cold water. Place beans in large pot with fresh water to cover generously. Cook until beans are tender but still slightly firm, about I 1/4 to I 1/2 hours. Drain in colander. Rinse again in cold water to prevent further cooking. Return drained beans to pot.

Meanwhile, sauté bacon until half cooked. Drain off fat. Add peppers, onion, garlic, cilantro, cumin and cayenne and sauté until peppers are crisp-tender. Add to beans. Add chicken broth and simmer until most of liquid is absorbed but bean mixture is still moist, about 30 to 40 minutes. Season to taste with salt and pepper. Add Italian dressing and toss. Chill. Stir well before serving.

6 servings. Each serving contains about: 461 calories; 2,590 mg sodium; 10 mg cholesterol; 27 grams fat; 31 grams carbohydrate; 25 grams protein; 2.32 grams fiber.

CHINESE CHICKEN SALAD

New Moon Restaurant, Los Angeles

The New Moon restaurant in the Garment District of Los Angeles has been serving this first-of-its-kind chicken salad for generations.

1 chicken (2 1/2 pounds), cut up
2 eggs, beaten
Cornstarch
1 tablespoon Asian sesame oil
Vegetable oil
1 package (6 3/4 ounces) rice sticks
1 tablespoon dry mustard
1 tablespoon water
1 1/2 tablespoons hoisin sauce
2 tablespoons soy sauce
Salt, pepper
1/2 cup cilantro leaves
1 bunch green onions, shredded
2 tablespoons toasted sesame seeds
3 tablespoons chopped toasted almonds
1 small head iceberg lettuce, finely shredded

Dip chicken pieces in egg to coat, then in cornstarch. Heat sesame oil and 2 tablespoons vegetable oil in heavy skillet. Fry chicken pieces until browned and tender. Drain on paper towels and cool. Bone and shred.

Heat oil for deep frying to 365 degrees. Fry rice sticks a small batch at a time until puffed, 1 to 2 seconds. Drain on paper towels.

Combine chicken and rice sticks in bowl. Mix dry mustard with water to make a paste. Add hoisin and soy sauces and season to taste with salt and pepper. Add to chicken mixture. Add cilantro, green onions, sesame seeds, almonds and lettuce and toss thoroughly. Serve immediately.

4 servings. Each serving contains about: 787 calories; 1,321 mg sodium; 229 mg cholesterol; 45 grams fat; 60 grams carbohydrate; 35 grams protein; 3.12 grams fiber.

BARBECUE CHICKEN SALAD

Panda Inn Restaurants

This is a cool, spicy and generous Chinese-style chicken salad.

SALAD:
Oil for deep frying
4 won ton wrappers, cut in strips
1/2 ounce rice noodles
1 1/3 cups shredded cooked chicken breast
3 cups shredded iceberg lettuce
1 tablespoon shredded pickled red ginger
1/4 cup shredded carrot
1/2 cup shredded cabbage
3 tablespoons sesame seeds

DRESSING:
1 cup sugar
3/4 cup rice vinegar
Juice of 1 lemon
2 teaspoons mushroom soy sauce
1/2 teaspoon salt

SALAD:
   Heat oil to 375 degrees. Fry won tons just until golden brown and crisp. Drain. Fry rice noodles until white and puffed. Drain and cool.
   Place chicken in large bowl. Top with lettuce, ginger, carrot, cabbage, won ton, noodles and sesame seeds. Pour 1/4 cup or more of dressing over salad and toss to coat ingredients well. (Reserve remaining dressing for future use.)

DRESSING:
   Blend sugar, vinegar, lemon juice, soy sauce and salt. Refrigerate in tightly covered container up to 1 month. Makes about 1 cup.

2 servings. Each serving, with dressing, contains about: 596 calories; 335 mg sodium; 62 mg cholesterol; 23 grams fat; 73 grams carbohydrate; 27 grams protein; 1.83 grams fiber.

SPINACH CHICKEN SALAD

Marmalade Cafe, Santa Monica

This is a delightful twist on an old and nutritious favorite.

SPINACH SALAD:
4 boneless chicken breasts
I red bell pepper
I green bell pepper
I yellow bell pepper
I carrot
3 stalks celery
2 pounds fresh spinach
I cup crumbled Gorgonzola cheese
1/2 cup walnuts, toasted and coarsely chopped

BALSAMIC DRESSING:
1/2 cup balsamic vinegar
2 shallots, roasted and chopped
2 cloves garlic, roasted and chopped
I teaspoon dried crushed red pepper
I teaspoon dried oregano
I teaspoon Italian seasoning
I 1/2 cups extra-virgin olive oil
Salt, pepper

SPINACH SALAD:
Grill chicken over high heat; let cool. Cut into bite-size pieces. (Chicken can be cooked up to 2 days in advance; wrap tightly and refrigerate.)

Seed bell peppers and cut into thin strips. Peel carrot and celery and cut into thin sticks. Clean and stem spinach.

Combine chicken, peppers, carrot and celery in large bowl. Add Balsamic Dressing and toss. Add spinach and toss. Sprinkle with cheese and walnuts.

BALSAMIC DRESSING:
Combine vinegar, shallots, garlic, red pepper, oregano and Italian seasoning in bowl and whisk until well blended. Add oil in steady stream, whisking rapidly until slightly thickened. Season to taste with salt and pepper. Makes about 2 cups.

◆◆◆

6 servings. Each serving, with dressing, contains about: 816 calories; 366 mg sodium; 74 mg cholesterol; 73 grams fat; 16 grams carbohydrate; 29 grams protein; 2.36 grams fiber.

❖ *Chef's Tip*: To roast whole heads of garlic, rub surface with damp cloth to remove dust and dirt. Dry with clean cloth and rub with oil. Roast in preheated 400-degree oven 10 to 15 minutes or until softened. To roast individual cloves of garlic or shallots, brush cloves with oil and bake at 400 degrees 4 to 5 minutes for garlic and 8 to 10 minutes for shallots, depending on size. Do not scorch.

CHICKEN SALAD with ORANGE SOUFFLÉ

Neiman Marcus, Beverly Hills

Neiman Marcus' chicken salad is famed. Served over orange soufflé in the store's Mariposa Cafe, it is also wonderful mounded in pineapple, papaya or avocado shells. The orange soufflé can be served separately as part of a salad, or can double as dessert.

ORANGE SOUFFLÉ:

2 envelopes unflavored gelatin
2 cups sugar
Pinch of salt
4 egg yolks
2 1/2 cups fresh orange juice (from about 10 oranges)
I teaspoon grated orange zest
I teaspoon grated lemon zest
3 tablespoons lemon juice
I cup orange sections, cut in half
2 cups whipping cream, whipped

CHICKEN SALAD:

I cup mayonnaise
Dash of wine vinegar
1/2 cup whipping cream
3 cups diced cooked chicken
1/2 cup diced celery
Salt, pepper
Toasted sliced almonds

ORANGE SOUFFLÉ:

Combine gelatin, sugar and salt in saucepan. Set aside.

Beat egg yolks with I cup orange juice. Stir into gelatin mixture. Cook over medium-low heat, stirring constantly, just until mixture comes to boil. Remove from heat. Stir in remaining orange juice with grated zest. Chill, stirring occasionally, until mixture mounds when dropped from spoon.

Stir in orange sections. Fold in whipped cream. Pour into 2-quart ring mold. Chill until set.

CHICKEN SALAD:

Mix mayonnaise, vinegar and cream. Add chicken and celery and toss to coat. Season to taste with salt and pepper.

Unmold Orange Soufflé onto round platter. Fill center of mold with Chicken Salad. Sprinkle with sliced almonds.

◆◆◆

8 servings. Each serving contains about: 748 calories; 363 mg sodium; 293 mg cholesterol; 44 grams fat; 70 grams carbohydrate; 21 grams protein; 0.21 gram fiber.

NO-MAYO ROASTED CHICKEN SALAD
Koo Koo Roo

Most chain operations are reluctant to part with their trade secrets, but not Koo Koo Roo. The chain is proud of this recipe for using fruits, nuts and balsamic vinegar to create a "fresh and tasty entree for all occasions."

I roasted chicken
14 to 16 red seedless grapes, quartered
2 stalks celery, diced
I cup toasted sliced almonds
2 tablespoons balsamic vinegar
1/4 cup olive oil
Salt, pepper

Remove bone, gristle, fat and skin from chicken and shred meat into 2-inch strips. Place chicken in large mixing bowl. You should have about 1 1/2 pounds.

Add grapes, celery, almonds, vinegar, and olive oil to chicken. Season with salt and pepper to taste. Mix well and chill until ready to serve.

4 servings. Each serving contains about: 561 calories; 629 mg sodium; 115 mg cholesterol; 40 grams fat; 124 grams carbohydrate; 41 grams protein; 1.3 grams fiber.

SAUCES

◆◆◆

Restaurant sauces and dressings are among the most difficult foods to reproduce because, more often than not, they fail when broken down from large-quantity batches. Chemical changes occur, and the sauce or dressing is no longer the same.

Yet some restaurants have courageously reproduced their prized recipes and sent us home-size recipes that do work. You'll find the most requested and most successful of these recipes in this chapter.

There are old and new recipes among them. Newer ones, such as the Loews Santa Monica Beach Hotel Herb Dressing, contain negligible calories, cholesterol and fat, a sure sign that today's readers are more health conscious than ever. But some older recipes, such as the mayonnaise-laden Honey Mustard Dressing from The Proud Bird, are still going strong. Benihana dressings and sauces have been top favorites for many years.

Herb Dressing ◆ Loews Santa Monica Beach Hotel

Honey Mustard Dressing ◆ The Proud Bird, Los Angeles

Creamed Horseradish ◆ Lawry's Prime Rib

Benihana Salad Dressing ◆ Benihana Restaurants

Minami Salad Dressing ◆ Minami Japanese Restaurant

Salsa ◆ El Torito Restaurants

Creamy Pesto Salad Dressing ◆ The Old Spaghetti Factory

Spaghetti Sauce ◆ Little Joe's

HERB DRESSING
Loews Santa Monica Beach Hotel, Santa Monica

Joe Cochran sent this recipe when he was executive chef at the hotel. His calorie- and fat-conscious dressings were popular with the lunch crowd.

I cup finely shredded peeled cucumber
I cup balsamic vinegar
1/4 cup minced garlic
1/4 cup chopped chives
1/4 cup chopped fresh dill
1/4 cup chopped fresh tarragon
1/4 cup chopped fresh basil
1/2 cup seeded, diced tomatoes
Salt

Combine cucumber, vinegar, garlic, chives, dill, tarragon, basil and tomatoes. Season to taste with salt. Serve with greens.

◆◆◆

About 2 1/4 cups or 10 servings. Each serving contains about: 14 calories; 33 mg sodium; 0 cholesterol; 0 fat; 4 grams carbohydrate; 2 grams protein; 0 fiber.

HONEY MUSTARD DRESSING

The Proud Bird, Los Angeles

We were pleased to discover that The Proud Bird, an old airport-area landmark, is alive and well, and so is this popular dressing.

3 cups mayonnaise
1/2 cup sugar
1/2 cup honey
1/4 cup prepared mustard, preferably French's
1/4 cup distilled white vinegar
1/4 cup minced onion
1/4 bunch parsley, chopped
I cup vegetable oil

Combine mayonnaise, sugar, honey, mustard, vinegar, onion and parsley. Blend in oil. Chill at least I hour before serving.

◆◆◆

About 4 cups or 32 servings. Each serving contains about: 127 calories; 41 mg sodium; I mg cholesterol; 9 grams fat; II grams carbohydrate; 0 protein; 0.21 gram fiber.

CREAMED HORSERADISH

Lawry's Prime Rib, Los Angeles

Let us introduce you to a wonderful recipe for creamed horseradish, shared by one of Los Angeles' oldest prime rib restaurants.

1 cup whipping cream
1 ounce horseradish root, peeled and grated or ground
1 teaspoon seasoned salt
2 or 3 drops hot pepper sauce

Whip cream until soft peaks form. Gradually add horseradish, seasoned salt and hot pepper sauce. Continue whipping until stiff. Refrigerate until ready to serve.

◆◆◆

2 cups. Each tablespoon contains about: 27 calories; 46 mg sodium; 10 mg cholesterol; 3 grams fat; 0 carbohydrate; 0 protein; 0.02 gram fiber.

BENIHANA SALAD DRESSING
Benihana Restaurants

Here's a very popular dressing from the national Benihana restaurant chain.

1/4 cup chopped onion
1/4 cup peanut oil
2 tablespoons rice vinegar
2 tablespoons water
I tablespoon chopped fresh ginger
I tablespoon chopped celery
I tablespoon soy sauce
I 1/2 teaspoons tomato paste
I 1/2 teaspoons sugar
I teaspoon lemon juice
Pinch each of salt and pepper

Combine onion, oil, vinegar, water, ginger, celery, soy sauce, tomato paste, sugar, lemon juice and salt and pepper in blender or food processor and blend until almost smooth. Store in refrigerator.

◆◆◆

6 servings. Each serving contains about: 98 calories; 276 mg sodium; 0 mg cholesterol; 9 grams fat; 5 grams carbohydrate; 0 protein; 0.13 gram fiber.

MINAMI SALAD DRESSING

Minami Japanese Restaurant, Omni Los Angeles Hotel

We get numerous requests for this zesty dressing, which is served on the typical green salad accompanying most teppan (Japanese grill) meals.

3/4 cup vegetable oil
1/4 cup rice vinegar
1 tablespoon soy sauce
1 egg yolk
1 teaspoon salt or to taste
1 tablespoon black pepper
1 tablespoon dry mustard
2 tablespoons paprika

Combine oil, vinegar, soy sauce, egg yolk, salt, pepper, dry mustard and paprika in bowl and beat until smooth and syrupy.

◆◆◆

About 1 1/2 cups. Each tablespoon contains about: 66 calories; 337 mg sodium; 11 mg cholesterol; 7 grams fat; 0 carbohydrate; 0 protein; 0.11 gram fiber.

❖ *Chef's Tip*: When raw egg is called for in a recipe, there are a couple of methods a cook can use to make safer. Here are two methods the *Times* Test Kitchen uses to heat egg yolks before using them in recipes that traditionally use raw yolks.

MICROWAVE METHOD: Heat yolks on HIGH 30 seconds. Now heat the yolks on HIGH at 10-second intervals, up to 60 seconds total cooking time, watching through window to see if yolks begin to move. As soon as movement is detected in yolks, heat on HIGH 8 to 10 seconds more. Beat yolks until smooth with fork or whisk. Return to microwave and heat on HIGH until yolks again begin to move, up to 10 seconds. Remove yolks from microwave, cover and let stand 1 minute. If using extra-large eggs, stir in 2 tablespoons plus 1 teaspoon water before microwaving.

STOVETOP METHOD: Heat 2 yolks over very low heat in saucepan with 1/4 cup of the most acidic liquid called for in the recipe. (The acidity in vinegars and lemon or lime juice helps prevent the yolks from curdling.) Stir the yolks constantly until they thicken like lemon curd, 3 to 4 minutes. If using cooking thermometer, check that yolks are heated to 160 degrees, or to 140 for 3 1/2 minutes.

SALSA

El Torito Restaurants

El Torito published this recipe in a promotional booklet sent to us a few years ago. A reader suggested spreading the salsa on tortillas with honey butter. We couldn't wait to try it.

2 cups diced tomatoes
1/2 cup diced onion
I to 2 tablespoons seeded and minced jalapeños
I tablespoon vegetable oil
I teaspoon distilled white vinegar
I teaspoon lime juice
1/2 teaspoon dried Mexican oregano
1/4 teaspoon salt or to taste
1/4 cup finely chopped cilantro

Combine tomatoes, onion, jalapeños, oil, vinegar, lime juice, oregano, salt and cilantro in large stainless steel bowl and mix well. Chill.

◆◆◆

6 servings. Each serving contains about: 4I calories; I05 mg sodium; 0 cholesterol; 3 grams fat; 5 grams carbohydrate; I gram protein; 0.6I gram fiber.

CREAMY PESTO SALAD DRESSING

The Old Spaghetti Factory, Los Angeles

The chef says that flavor is enhanced when the dressing is refrigerated overnight.

3/4 cup vegetable oil
I cup mayonnaise
3/4 cup buttermilk
2 tablespoons grated Romano cheese
2 tablespoons crushed dried basil
1/2 teaspoon salt
I clove garlic, minced
Hot pepper sauce

Whisk together oil and mayonnaise. Add buttermilk, cheese, basil, salt, garlic and hot pepper sauce to taste and mix thoroughly. Cover and refrigerate overnight to blend flavors.

◆◆◆

2 1/2 cups. Each 2-tablespoon serving contains about: 125 calories; 164 mg sodium; 4 mg cholesterol; 13 grams fat; 3 grams carbohydrate; I gram protein; 0 fiber.

SPAGHETTI SAUCE

Little Joe's, Los Angeles

Our readers still request this recipe, even though the former downtown Los Angeles landmark is long gone.

3 tablespoons olive oil
1 medium onion
2 tablespoons minced green bell pepper
1 stalk celery, chopped
1 clove garlic, minced
1 can (1 pound 12 ounces) whole tomatoes, chopped
1 can (1 pound 12 ounces) tomato puree
1 tablespoon dried basil
1 tablespoon crushed dried oregano
1 bay leaf
1/2 cup dry red wine
1 cup water
2 teaspoons salt
1/2 teaspoon black pepper
2 tablespoons freshly grated Parmesan cheese

Heat oil in large heavy pot. Add onion, green pepper, celery and garlic and sauté until vegetables are tender. Add tomatoes, tomato puree, basil, oregano and bay leaf and simmer 1 hour, stirring frequently. Add wine, water, salt and pepper and simmer 1 hour longer. If sauce is too thick, add more water. When sauce is cooked, add Parmesan cheese and mix well.

◆◆◆

12 servings. Each serving contains about: 90 calories; 538 mg sodium; 1 mg cholesterol; 4 grams fat; 11 grams carbohydrate; 2 grams protein; 0.98 gram fiber.

EGGS & CHEESE

◆◆◆

In the 1970s eggs and cheese became virtually taboo because of their alleged link to heart disease. For years readers shunned them, and so did "Culinary SOS," which depended on reader requests. But today experts say that, eaten in moderation, eggs—nature's low-calorie, low-cost nutrient bomb in a package—are probably good for you. It is estimated that a family of four can safely consume a dozen eggs per week. For those on a fat- and cholesterol-restricted diet, though, one or two eggs per week per person are enough. Still, those on a restricted diet should consult their physicians.

Now that eggs are back in favor, readers who remember the great egg and cheese dishes of yesteryear want them again. So we have been digging into our dusty files to retrieve the tattered and torn recipes. Here are some favorites from famous restaurants (some of them now gone) that have stood the test of time.

Welsh Rabbit ◆ Cock 'n' Bull

Quiche Lorraine ◆ The Broadway Department Store

Machaca Burrito ◆ Catering Truck

Chiles Rellenos ◆ El Cholo

Herbed Scrambled Eggs ◆ The Plum Pudding

Quiche à la Ma Maison ◆ Ma Maison

Délices au Gruyère ◆ Swiss Cafe

Eggs in a Peg ◆ Citrus

Garden Cheese Pie ◆ Knott's Berry Farm

WELSH RABBIT

Cock 'n' Bull, Hollywood

The Cock 'n' Bull restaurant on the Sunset Strip in Hollywood is gone, but the memory of its outstanding Welsh rabbit lingers.

1 1/2 cups milk
1 pound aged Cheddar cheese, diced
1/4 cup (1/2 stick) butter, plus extra for English muffins
1/2 cup all-purpose flour
1 teaspoon dry mustard
Cayenne pepper
1/4 teaspoon salt
3/4 cup beer
2 teaspoons Worcestershire sauce
2 teaspoons steak sauce
2 dashes hot pepper sauce
6 English muffins

Heat milk in top of double boiler over simmering water. Add cheese and stir until melted.

Melt butter in skillet. Sift flour into butter and add dry mustard, cayenne to taste and salt. Stir until mixture forms a smooth paste.

Gradually add milk-cheese mixture and cook 10 minutes, stirring constantly. Stir in beer, Worcestershire sauce, steak sauce and hot pepper sauce. Keep warm until serving time.

Split muffins and butter cut sides; grill or toast. Serve sauce over muffins.

6 servings. Each serving contains about: 598 calories; 1,104 mg sodium; 105 mg cholesterol; 36 grams fat; 39 grams carbohydrate; 27 grams protein; 0.07 gram fiber.

QUICHE LORRAINE

The Broadway Department Store, Los Angeles

The old Broadway department store was a haven for homespun recipes that readers raved about and used frequently in their everyday cooking and entertaining. This is one of them.

5 eggs
2/3 cup sour cream
Salt, pepper
Nutmeg
1 cup whipping cream
3/4 cup shredded Swiss cheese
1 unbaked 10-inch pie shell
6 to 7 slices bacon, cooked and crumbled

Beat eggs in bowl. Add sour cream and mix until smooth. Strain mixture. Season to taste with salt, pepper and nutmeg. Add cream and mix well.

Preheat oven to 300 degrees. Spread half of Swiss cheese in unbaked pie shell. Layer crumbled bacon over cheese and top with remaining cheese. Pour in sour cream mixture. Bake 1 hour or until custard is golden brown and set. Serve hot.

◆◆◆

8 servings. Each serving contains about: 443 calories; 270 mg sodium; 194 mg cholesterol; 36 grams fat; 19 grams carbohydrate; 11 grams protein; 0.06 gram fiber.

MACHACA BURRITO

Catering Truck, Downtown Los Angeles

We discovered Dinora Guzman, a catering truck cook in the Garment District in downtown Los Angeles, as she prepared dozens of these burritos for hungry people on their way to work. This burrito makes a great breakfast party dish.

BURRITO:
Lard, butter or margarine
8 ounces round steak, diced
1 teaspoon dry mustard
Seasoned salt
Freshly ground pepper
1 to 2 teaspoons Worcestershire sauce
1 small onion, diced
1/2 green bell pepper, diced
1 tomato, diced
6 eggs, lightly beaten
6 flour tortillas

MEXICAN BEANS (OPTIONAL):
1 cup dried pinto beans, well rinsed
1/2 teaspoon salt
Pinch of ground cumin
Pinch of chile powder
1/2 cup vegetable oil

BURRITO:

Grease griddle or skillet with lard. Add beef. Season to taste with dry mustard, seasoned salt and pepper. Sprinkle with Worcestershire. Sauté until browned and done as desired. Remove meat and set aside.

Melt 1 tablespoon lard in same skillet. Add onion and green pepper and sauté until onion is tender. Add tomato and sauté until tender. Add eggs and scramble. Add meat mixture and toss until heated through.

Heat tortillas on griddle to warm and soften. Top each tortilla with some of egg and meat mixture. Top with beans, if desired. Fold in sides of tortilla and roll to make neat package. Serve for eating out of hand for breakfast or lunch.

MEXICAN BEANS:

Place beans in saucepan and cover generously with water. Let soak 6 to 8 hours or overnight. Drain and generously cover with water again. Bring to boil, cover and boil gently 45 minutes. Add salt, cumin and chile powder and cook until beans are tender, about 15 minutes longer. Drain beans, reserving cooking liquid.

Heat oil in skillet. Add beans and some of bean cooking liquid. Partially mash beans, leaving some whole. Cook until mixture is thick. Makes 2 cups.

◆◆◆

6 burritos. Each, without beans, contains about: 306 calories; 236 mg sodium; 326 mg cholesterol; 16 grams fat; 18 grams carbohydrate; 22 grams protein; 2.19 grams fiber.

8 servings of beans. Each serving contains about: 150 calories; 148 mg sodium; 0 cholesterol; 14 grams fat; 6 grams carbohydrate; 2 grams protein; 0.66 gram fiber.

CHILES RELLENOS

El Cholo, Los Angeles

This dish is among the most popular at the venerable El Cholo.

CHILES:
6 eggs, separated
Pinch of salt
6 canned whole green chiles
9 ounces shredded Cheddar or Monterey Jack cheese
Shortening for deep frying

RELLENO SAUCE:
1 cup chopped onion
1/2 cup chopped green bell pepper
1/8 teaspoon minced garlic
2 tablespoons vegetable oil
2 cans (1 pound each) whole tomatoes, cut up
1/2 teaspoon salt
1/8 teaspoon pepper
1/4 teaspoon dried oregano

CHILES:

Beat egg yolks in large bowl. Using clean beaters, beat egg whites with salt until stiff. Fold into beaten yolks. Stuff each chile with 3 tablespoons cheese.

Heat shortening in large skillet. Drop heaping tablespoon of egg mixture into hot shortening and spread with back of spoon. Place a stuffed chile on egg mixture and cover with another spoonful of egg, sealing batter around chile.

Fry until puffy and browned on each side, turning gently. Drain on paper towels and keep hot while frying remaining chiles. Serve with Relleno Sauce.

RELLENO SAUCE:

Sauté onion, green pepper and garlic in oil until onion is tender. Add tomatoes, salt, pepper and oregano. Cover and simmer 15 minutes. Makes 4 cups.

6 servings. Each serving, with sauce, contains about: 384 calories; 777 mg sodium; 291 mg cholesterol; 29 grams fat; 12 grams carbohydrate; 20 grams protein; 2.24 grams fiber.

HERBED SCRAMBLED EGGS

The Plum Pudding, Brookings, Oregon

The scrambled eggs at The Plum Pudding had our reader scrambling for a recipe.

12 large eggs
1/2 cup imitation sour cream
1 1/2 teaspoons chopped fresh basil leaves
1/4 teaspoon minced garlic
2 tablespoons butter or margarine

Whisk eggs with imitation sour cream, basil and garlic. Melt butter in skillet over medium heat. Add egg mixture and scramble to desired doneness. Serve immediately.

◆◆◆

6 servings. Each serving contains about: 219 calories; 199 mg sodium; 503 mg cholesterol; 15 grams fat; 3 grams carbohydrate; 16 grams protein; 0 grams fiber.

QUICHE à la MA MAISON

Ma Maison, West Hollywood

In its heyday, Ma Maison attracted the famous and infamous not only because of its charming host, Patrick Terrail, and a unique garden setting, but also because the food was good. (Wolfgang Puck and Guy Leroy were the chefs.) Quiche à la Ma Maison was a favorite on the lunch menu.

Puff pastry or pie pastry dough for 10-inch quiche pan
8 ounces bacon, diced
6 ounces ham, diced
1/4 cup chopped fresh chives
1/2 cup coarsely grated Gruyère cheese
7 large eggs
3 cups half and half or whipping cream
1/4 teaspoon nutmeg
1/4 teaspoon salt
1/2 teaspoon white pepper

Preheat oven to 350 degrees. Grease 10-inch quiche pan and line with pastry or pie dough, rolling to fit pan. Do not trim edges.

Line pastry with wax paper and fill with dried beans or pie weights. Bake crust until lightly browned, about 12 minutes. Remove wax paper and beans.

Meanwhile, cook bacon until crisp; drain on paper towel. Spread evenly in baked pie shell. Add ham, chives and cheese. Beat eggs with half and half, nutmeg, salt and pepper until well blended. Pour into shell. Trim edges of shell. Bake until custard is puffed and browned, 30 to 40 minutes. Serve hot.

◆◆◆

6 servings. Each serving contains about: 660 calories; 1413 mg sodium; 388 mg cholesterol; 50 grams fat; 17 grams carbohydrate; 36 grams protein; 0.16 grams fiber.

DÉLICES au GRUYÈRE

Swiss Cafe, Beverly Hills

Délices au Gruyère was one of our most requested recipes when the former Swiss Cafe in Beverly Hills was in its prime about 30 years ago.

1/4 cup (1/2 stick) butter or margarine
All-purpose flour
1 1/2 cups milk, heated
Salt, pepper
8 ounces Gruyère cheese, grated
3 egg yolks, beaten
1 egg
1/4 cup milk
1 tablespoon vegetable oil
Fine dry bread crumbs
Oil for deep frying

Melt butter in saucepan over low heat. Blend in 5 tablespoons flour and cook, stirring, until mixture is golden. Add hot milk and cook, stirring, until sauce is smooth and thick. Cook over low heat 8 to 10 minutes longer. Season to taste with salt and pepper. Add cheese and stir until melted.

Stir egg yolks into sauce and cook, stirring, 3 minutes, being careful not to let sauce boil.

Grease shallow 12 x 7-inch pan. Spread mixture in pan and let cool, then cover with wax paper and chill.

Cut mixture into 10 or more equal portions and form each into ball or cone. Roll in flour, then in egg beaten with 1/4 cup milk and 1 tablespoon oil. Drain on paper towels, then roll in crumbs.

Heat oil to 370 degrees. Fry croquettes until golden on all sides, 1 to 1 1/2 minutes. Drain on paper towels. Serve hot as a luncheon dish with a favorite tomato sauce or plain as an appetizer.

6 servings. Each serving contains about: 417 calories; 336 mg sodium; 220 mg cholesterol; 33 grams fat; 13 grams carbohydrate; 18 grams protein; 0.22 grams fiber.

EGGS in a PEG

Citrus, Los Angeles

Many coffee shops, cafeterias, drugstore counters and restaurants once served Eggs in a Peg. At Citrus, the eggs are served over ham and covered with hollandaise sauce for a lovely variation on eggs Benedict.

4 slices bread
2 tablespoons butter
4 eggs
2 slices American cheese, cut into strips (optional)
Salt, pepper

Cut round, silver-dollar-size hole in each bread slice. Melt butter in skillet. Lightly brown bread on each side. Break 1 egg into center of each piece of bread and fry gently, covered.

When eggs are partially cooked, place strip of cheese over them, cover and let cheese melt. Season to taste with salt and pepper.

◆◆◆

4 servings. Each serving, with cheese topping, contains about: 193 calories; 322 mg sodium; 229 mg cholesterol; 12 grams fat; 13 grams carbohydrate; 8 grams protein.

GARDEN CHEESE PIE

Knott's Berry Farm, Garden Grove

This cheese pie makes a nourishing luncheon or late supper dish.

1 9-inch unbaked pie shell
1 1/2 tablespoons diced red onion
1/4 cup diced celery
1/4 cup chopped cauliflower
3/4 cup shredded Swiss cheese
3/4 cup shredded Cheddar cheese
4 eggs, beaten
1/2 cup plus 2 tablespoons half and half

Preheat oven to 400 degrees. Bake pie shell 10 minutes. Set aside.

Reduce oven heat to 275 degrees. Combine onion, celery and cauliflower in small bowl and mix well. In another bowl combine cheeses and mix well. In a third bowl, combine eggs with half and half and beat 2 minutes. Evenly layer 1/3 of cheese mixture, all of vegetable mixture and another 1/3 of cheese mixture in pie shell. Pour egg mixture evenly over filling.

Bake until crust and filling are golden, about 55 minutes. Top with remaining 1/3 of cheese mixture and bake 5 minutes longer. Let stand 10 minutes before cutting and serving.

◆◆◆

6 servings. Each serving contains about: 312 calories; 337 mg sodium; 202 mg cholesterol; 22 grams fat; 14 grams carbohydrate; 15 grams protein; 0.20 grams fiber.

SEAFOOD

◆◆◆

There was a time in Los Angeles when seafood dishes were a mere footnote on restaurant menus. Today restaurants offer more seafood than ever, and the number that have made their name by specializing in seafood has skyrocketed.

Part of the reason for this may be concerns about fat and cholesterol. With nutrition experts touting the health benefits of fish, converts to it have grown in number, as have restaurants filling the demand. Technological advances that allow fresh fish to be rushed to market overnight from around the world have also brought wider variety and a new taste for certain fish and shellfish. Green mussels and John Dory from New Zealand, tiger shrimp from Thailand, mullet from the Red Sea, branzino from Italian Adriatic waters became immediate favorites once they were available in this country.

In this sunny climate for fish, "Culinary SOS" became flooded with requests for fish dishes; they have become some of the most frequently requested recipes over recent years. By far, salmon seems to be the clear reader favorite. It is featured here in several recipes, including a salmon burger, which could become as much a favorite as hamburger.

Cioppino ◆ Far Niente

Shrimp Enchilada ◆ El Chaya

Seafood Chow Mein ◆ Mon Kee

Paella ◆ Chaya Venice

Enchiladas Santa Barbara ◆ El Cholo

Halibut in Lime Caper Butter ◆ Newport Landing

Marinated Salmon and Bliss Potato Salad ◆ Patinette Cafe at MOCA

Salmon Burgers ◆ Clifton's

Salmon with Papaya Sauce ◆ Cha Cha Cha, Encino

Pescado Stew ◆ Can Cun

Stuffed Trout ◆ Velvet Turtle

CIOPPINO
Far Niente, Glendale

Far Niente was good enough to mention that this dish is not on the menu but is served on special order. This cioppino is thick enough to serve over pasta, which is exactly how it's done at Far Niente. Or you can make a soup of it, using any combination of seafood you like.

2 tablespoons olive oil
5 mussels
5 cockles
3 large shrimp, shell on
4 calamari (squid), cleaned and sliced
1/4 cup bay scallops
3 cloves garlic, chopped
2 tablespoons chopped fresh parsley
1/4 teaspoon dried red pepper flakes
1/4 cup (about) dry white wine
2 cups tomato sauce
4 ounces spaghetti or other pasta, cooked

   Heat olive oil in 10-inch skillet over high heat until it smokes. Carefully add mussels, cockles, shrimp, calamari, scallops, garlic, parsley and pepper flakes and sauté until all shells are open, about 3 minutes, stirring twice. Add 1/4 cup wine and cover. Cook 1 minute. Add tomato sauce. Cover, then shake and stir over medium heat until bubbly and hot, 3 to 5 minutes. If sauce appears too thick, add 2 table-spoons wine. Serve over cooked pasta.

◆◆◆

2 servings. Each serving contains about: 503 calories; 1,902 mg sodium; 167 mg cholesterol; 18 grams fat; 43 grams carbohydrate; 40 grams protein; 1.98 grams fiber.

SHRIMP ENCHILADA

El Chaya, West Hollywood

You can serve Shrimp Enchilada as an appetizer or a main course.

2 tablespoons olive oil
1/2 cup diced onion
I cup diced tomato
40 medium shrimp, deveined, peeled and halved
I bunch cilantro, stemmed
I jalapeño, chopped
2 shallots, minced
3 cloves garlic, minced
I cup heavy whipping cream
1/2 cup shredded Monterey Jack cheese
8 flour tortillas

Heat olive oil in skillet over medium-high heat. Add onion and tomato and sauté until onion is tender. Stir in shrimp and cook just until they turn pink.

Combine cilantro, jalapeño, shallots and garlic in blender or food processor and blend to form paste. Add I tablespoon water if needed to blend ingredients. Set aside.

Combine cream and cheese in saucepan and place over low heat just until cheese melts. Set aside.

Preheat oven to 350 degrees. Evenly spread shrimp mixture on each tortilla and roll. Spread half of cilantro sauce on bottom of rectangular baking dish to cover. Arrange rolled tortillas in dish and pour remaining cilantro sauce over. Bake about 10 minutes to heat through. Pour cheese sauce over enchiladas. Bake about 5 minutes longer, then broil until lightly browned.

4 servings. Each serving contains about: 620 calories; 594 mg sodium; 267 mg cholesterol; 39 grams fat; 34 grams carbohydrate; 32 grams protein; 0.71 gram fiber.

SEAFOOD CHOW MEIN

Mon Kee, Los Angeles

Here's a chow mein you've probably never tasted before. It's loaded with shrimp, scallops and squid.

2 quarts water
1 pound fresh egg noodles
9 tablespoons (about) vegetable or peanut oil
1 egg
4 to 6 medium shrimp, shelled and deveined
4 scallops, sliced
4 small squid, cleaned and sliced
1 green onion, cut into 1-inch pieces
2 cups thinly sliced Chinese greens (such as bok choy)
10 snow peas
1/2 cup chicken broth or bouillon
1/2 teaspoon sugar
1 teaspoon Chinese oyster sauce
1/4 teaspoon salt
1 tablespoon cornstarch mixed with 2 tablespoons water

Bring water to boil in large pot. Add noodles, stirring to separate, and return to boil 1 minute. Drain noodles. Rinse in cold water and drain well. Pat dry with paper towels.

Heat 3 tablespoons oil in wok over high heat. When hot, add 1/3 of noodles and spread evenly over bottom without disturbing. Cook until golden brown on bottom, about 5 to 6 minutes. Carefully turn and brown other side. Remove from wok and drain on paper towels. Transfer noodles to serving platter and pull apart slightly with hands. Keep warm. Repeat with remaining noodles in two more batches, adding 1 to 2 tablespoons oil each time.

Beat egg lightly in bowl. Add shrimp, scallops and squid, tossing to coat. Reheat wok over high heat. Add 3 tablespoons oil, swirling pan to coat sides. Add green onion, shrimp, scallops and squid and stir-fry 30 seconds; remove. Add 1 tablespoon oil to wok and reheat. Add Chinese greens and snow peas and stir-fry 1 minute.

Combine chicken broth, sugar, oyster sauce and salt. Add to wok with shrimp mixture. Add cornstarch paste and stir until slightly thickened. Serve over pan-fried noodles.

◆◆◆

6 servings. Each serving contains about: 520 calories; 303 mg sodium; 137 mg cholesterol; 26 grams fat; 58 grams carbohydrate; 15 grams protein; 0.68 gram fiber.

PAELLA
Chaya Venice, Venice

This meal in a dish needs only a simple lettuce-and-tomato salad and a good beer to wash it all down. For dessert, try a light coffee gelatin or chiffon-type cheesecake.

2 tablespoons light olive oil
5 tablespoons baby shrimp
3 tablespoons baby scallops
1/4 cup diced calamari (squid)
1/4 cup diced cooked baby octopus
1/4 cup diced chicken
3 tablespoons diced swordfish
3 tablespoons chopped shallot
1/4 cup chopped onion
I tablespoon chopped anchovy
3/4 cup Japanese short-grain rice
3/4 cup long-grain rice
1/2 cup white wine
I cup water
1/8 teaspoon saffron mixed with 1/2 cup water
I cup chicken broth
1/2 cup bottled clam juice
1/2 cup tomato sauce
8 to 10 littleneck clams
4 New Zealand mussels
4 large shrimp, shelled
4 whole sea scallops
2 tablespoons garlic-flavored oil
8 Kalamata olives
Salt, pepper
Chopped fresh parsley
Lemon wedges (garnish)

Preheat oven to 500 degrees. Heat olive oil in paella pan or flameproof casserole. Add baby shrimp, baby scallops, calamari, octopus, chicken and swordfish and sauté until lightly cooked. Add shallot, onion and anchovy and sauté until onion is barely tender. Increase heat and add short- and long-grain rice, wine, water, saffron mixture, chicken broth, clam juice and tomato sauce. Simmer over high heat 8 minutes. Add littleneck clams and mussels.

Bake seafood mixture 8 minutes. Add large shrimp, sea scallops, garlic-flavored oil and olives and bake 8 minutes longer. Season to taste with salt and pepper. Sprinkle with parsley and garnish with lemon wedges.

◆◆◆

4 servings. Each serving contains about: 601 calories; 1,169 mg sodium; 128 mg cholesterol; 20 grams fat; 62 grams carbohydrate; 36 grams protein; 1.01 grams fiber.

ENCHILADAS SANTA BARBARA
El Cholo, La Habra

Most markets carry the dried New Mexico and guajillo chiles called for here, but a milder variety, like the California dried chile, may be substituted.

GUAJILLO CHILE SAUCE:
3 cups water
1 ounce dried New Mexico chiles, stemmed and seeded
2 ounces dried guajillo chiles, stemmed and seeded
1 tablespoon vegetable oil
1/4 cup chopped onion
1 tomato, seeded and chopped
1 large clove garlic, minced
1/2 teaspoon dried oregano
1/4 teaspoon ground cumin
Salt

ENCHILADAS:
1/4 cup (1/2 stick) butter
6 ounces mushrooms, chopped (about 2 cups)
1 1/4 pounds chicken breast, chopped
1 1/4 pounds shelled raw shrimp, chopped
Pinch of salt
1 pound Monterey Jack cheese, grated
12 corn tortillas

GUAJILLO CHILE SAUCE:
Bring water and chiles to boil in heavy saucepan. Reduce heat, cover and simmer until chiles are tender, about 30 minutes. Drain, reserving chiles and cooking liquid separately.

Heat 1 1/2 teaspoons oil in medium saucepan over low heat. Add onion and sauté until golden, about 6 minutes. Add tomato, garlic, oregano, cumin and salt to taste and cook 5 minutes more.

Transfer mixture to blender. Add chiles and 2 cups reserved cooking liquid and puree until smooth.

Heat remaining oil in same saucepan over high heat. Add puree and boil 5 minutes, stirring constantly, adding more reserved cooking liquid to thin sauce if necessary.

ENCHILADAS:

Melt butter in skillet over medium heat. Add mushrooms, chicken and shrimp and cook 5 minutes. Add 2/3 cup Guajillo Chile Sauce to pan, coating chicken meat and mushrooms evenly. Simmer until chicken is cooked through, 3 to 5 minutes. Season with salt.

Preheat oven to 375 degrees. Top each tortilla with 1/4 cup grated cheese; top cheese with 1/2 cup filling. Roll tortillas and place seam side down in 13 x 9-inch baking dish. Top enchiladas with remaining sauce, then with remaining cheese.

Bake until heated through and cheese has melted, 12 to 15 minutes. Serve hot.

◆◆◆

6 servings. Each serving contains about: 700 calories; 868 mg sodium; 208 mg cholesterol; 38 grams fat; 43 grams carbohydrate; 50 grams protein; 6.25 grams fiber.

HALIBUT in LIME CAPER BUTTER

Newport Landing, Newport Beach

The chef's trick for keeping the halibut moist is to use egg wash and high temperatures when sautéing the fish. Another secret is the herb butter.

FISH:

1 cup all-purpose flour
Salt, pepper
6 Alaskan or Canadian halibut fillets, 8 ounces each
4 eggs
2 tablespoons milk
1/4 cup clarified butter
1 cup dry white wine, such as Chardonnay
1 jar (4 ounces) capers
1/4 cup lime juice

HERB BUTTER:

1/8 teaspoon seasoned salt
1/8 teaspoon white pepper
1/8 teaspoon garlic powder
1/8 teaspoon nutmeg
1/8 teaspoon crushed dried thyme
1/8 teaspoon crushed dried Greek oregano
1/8 teaspoon crushed dried marjoram
1/8 teaspoon crushed dried basil
1/8 teaspoon ground dried rosemary
1 teaspoon chopped fresh parsley
Dash of Worcestershire sauce
2 tablespoons lemon juice
1/2 teaspoon minced shallot
1/2 cup clarified butter

FISH:

Season flour with salt and pepper. Dredge halibut fillets in seasoned flour. Beat eggs with milk in shallow bowl and dip fillets in egg wash.

Preheat oven to 400 degrees. On stovetop, heat clarified butter in large ovenproof skillet over high heat until butter reaches smoke point. Brown fillets in butter, turning once, 1 to 2 minutes per side. Place skillet in oven and bake fillets until fish yields slightly and flakes when tested with fork or finger, 8 to 10 minutes.

Bring wine to boil in medium saucepan over medium heat and cook until reduced by half. Add capers and lime juice. Add Herb Butter and whisk to form lightly thickened sauce.

Remove fish from oven and pour sauce over. Return to oven and let sauce bubble 2 to 3 minutes.

HERB BUTTER:

Add salt, white pepper, garlic powder, nutmeg, thyme, oregano, marjoram, basil, rosemary, parsley, Worcestershire sauce, lemon juice and shallot to clarified butter and mix well.

◆◆◆

6 servings. Each serving contains about: 507 calories; 674 mg sodium; 262 mg cholesterol; 31 grams fat; 7 grams carbohydrate; 43 grams protein; 0.04 gram fiber.

MARINATED SALMON
and BLISS POTATO SALAD

Patinette Cafe at MOCA (Museum of Contemporary Art), Los Angeles

This is a cool, inviting dish for a summer menu.

2 pounds red Bliss potatoes
1/4 cup thinly sliced green onions
I tablespoon finely grated red radish
I tablespoon chopped fresh parsley
1/2 cup mayonnaise
I tablespoon grated horseradish
2 tablespoons prepared whole-grain mustard
Salt
White pepper
8 ounces thinly sliced marinated smoked salmon
2 tablespoons crème fraîche
I tablespoon chopped chives

Cook potatoes in boiling water just until tender. Drain and cool, then peel and cut into quarters.

Combine green onions, radish, parsley, mayonnaise, horseradish and mustard. Add potatoes and toss to coat well. Season to taste with salt and white pepper.

When ready to serve, divide salad among four plates. Cover each with 2 ounces salmon. Garnish top of salmon with dollop of crème fraîche and sprinkling of chives.

4 servings. Each serving contains about: 387 calories; 1,615 mg sodium; 24 mg cholesterol; 14 grams

❖ *Chef's Tip*: To create an 8-ounce marinated smoked salmon fillet, combine I tablespoon each diced onion, carrot and leek (white portion only), I teaspoon sugar and I teaspoon salt. Sprinkle over salmon fillet, coating well. Combine grated zest of 1/2 lemon, 1/4 teaspoon white pepper and 1/8 teaspoon ground coriander and sprinkle over salmon. Cover with plastic wrap and refrigerate up to 24 hours. Barbecue over medium-hot coals or grill until salmon is cooked through, about 3 to 5 minutes on each side. If a smoke oven is available, smoke according to manufacturer's directions. Carefully slice as directed in recipe.

SALMON BURGERS

Clifton's, Los Angeles

We broke down Clifton's large-quantity recipe, which means that the texture may not exactly resemble the original. But it shouldn't be too far off in flavor.

I 1/2 pounds salmon fillets, cooked and flaked, or 2 cans (I pound each) salmon
Juice of I lemon
I tablespoon chopped chives
1/4 cup chopped fresh parsley
I tablespoon dry mustard
1/2 teaspoon dried dill
1/4 cup freshly grated Parmesan cheese
3 cups fine dry bread crumbs
1/2 cup mayonnaise
3/4 cup chicken broth
I tablespoon paprika
12 tablespoons tartar sauce
1/4 cup (1/2 stick) butter, melted

Break salmon into small flakes in mixing bowl. Add lemon juice, chives, parsley, dry mustard, dill, Parmesan cheese, 2 cups bread crumbs and mayonnaise and mix well. Blend in enough chicken broth to moisten mixture.

Form mixture into 12 burgers. Arrange burgers on wax paper–lined tray and refrigerate at least I hour to blend flavors.

Mix remaining I cup bread crumbs with paprika in mixing bowl.

Preheat oven to 350 degrees. Arrange salmon burgers in greased baking pan. Using spatula, spread a tablespoon of tartar sauce over each burger, completely covering top surface. Sprinkle with crumb-paprika mixture and drizzle with melted butter. Bake until browned, about 20 minutes. Serve hot.

◆◆◆

12 servings. Each serving contains about: 310 calories; 440 mg sodium; 48 mg cholesterol; 19 grams fat; 14 grams carbohydrate; 20 grams protein; 0.41 gram fiber.

SALMON with PAPAYA SAUCE

Cha Cha Cha, Encino

You might want to serve this hot and spicy fish dish with rice, a beautiful green salad and, perhaps, a chilled white Chilean wine.

1/2 cup dry white wine
Juice of 2 lemons
Juice of 2 limes
4 tablespoons chopped garlic
Grated zest and juice of 1 orange
2 sprigs fresh dill, chopped
2 sprigs fresh thyme, chopped
Pinch of ground cumin
Black pepper
6 slices salmon fillet, 9 ounces each
2 tablespoons olive oil
1 tablespoon Hungarian paprika
3/4 teaspoon curry powder
Salt
2/3 cup chicken broth
1/2 bunch fresh oregano, chopped
1/4 cup (1/2 stick) unsalted butter
1 ripe papaya, peeled and sliced
1/2 bunch fresh basil, chopped
1/4 cup shredded coconut

Combine wine, lemon and lime juice, 2 tablespoons chopped garlic, orange zest and juice, dill, thyme, cumin and a pinch of pepper in shallow pan. Add salmon, cover and marinate in refrigerator several hours, turning several times.

Grill or broil marinated salmon just until fish flakes easily with fork, about 5 minutes on each side.

Heat olive oil. Add remaining 2 tablespoons chopped garlic, 1 teaspoon pepper, paprika, curry powder and salt to taste. Stir with wooden spoon 1 minute. Add chicken broth and oregano and boil until reduced by half. Add butter, papaya and basil and pour over salmon. Serve topped with sprinkling of coconut.

6 servings. Each serving contains about: 509 calories; 246 mg sodium; 109 mg cholesterol; 27 grams fat; 12 grams carbohydrate; 51 grams protein; 0.87 gram fiber.

PESCADO STEW
Can Cun, Pico Rivera

This straightforward stew will appeal to fish lovers, busy people and calorie counters.

2 tablespoons olive oil
1 small onion, minced
2 cloves garlic, minced
1 can (8 ounces) tomato sauce
5 cups water
1 teaspoon salt
1 bay leaf
2 carrots, thinly sliced
1/4 large cabbage, cubed
1 teaspoon garlic powder
1 1/2 pounds sea bass fillet, cut into pieces
2 tablespoons chopped cilantro

Heat oil in large saucepan. Add onion and garlic and sauté until tender, 1 to 2 minutes. Add tomato sauce, water, salt, bay leaf, carrots and cabbage and bring to boil. Reduce heat and simmer 5 minutes. Add fish and simmer 5 minutes longer. Sprinkle with cilantro.

4 servings. Each serving contains about: 250 calories; 1,051 mg sodium; 109 mg cholesterol; 10 grams fat; 14 grams carbohydrate; 26 grams protein; 1.39 grams fiber.

STUFFED TROUT

Velvet Turtle, Los Angeles

An excellent fish dish for company because much of it can be assembled ahead.

SHRIMP STUFFING:

2 tablespoons butter
I large onion, chopped
3 cups sliced mushrooms
I teaspoon salt
I teaspoon white pepper
1/4 cup diced red bell pepper
1/4 cup diced green onions
8 ounces cooked bay shrimp
2 cups dry sherry

TROUT:

6 to 8 whole trout (8 to 10 ounces each), boned
All-purpose flour
2 eggs, beaten
2 cups fine dry bread crumbs
1/4 cup (1/2 stick) butter
Juice and grated zest of I lemon
Salt, pepper

SHRIMP STUFFING:

Melt butter in large skillet over medium-high heat and sauté onion and mushrooms until lightly browned. Add salt, white pepper, red pepper, green onions, shrimp and sherry and simmer over medium heat until liquid is reduced to glaze, stirring occasionally. Let cool.

TROUT:

Dredge each trout in flour, dip in egg, then roll in bread crumbs to coat lightly.

Carefully fill each trout cavity with Shrimp Stuffing. Secure seams with wooden picks. Melt butter in large skillet. Sauté trout in butter, a few at a time, until lightly browned on both sides and stuffing is hot. Remove trout and keep warm.

Add lemon juice and zest to butter remaining in pan and heat a few seconds.

Season to taste with salt and pepper. Pour over trout.

◆◆◆

6 servings. Each serving contains about: 564 calories; 882 mg sodium; 255 mg cholesterol; 21 grams fat; 36 grams carbohydrate; 47 grams protein; 1.89 grams fiber.

POULTRY

◆◆◆

The "Culinary SOS" column has been answering requests for more poultry dishes than ever since health experts of the 1970s and 1980s started cautioning Americans against eating too much red meat and advising us to include more chicken and fish in our diet.

Restaurateurs, of course, were quick to meet the demand of diet-conscious diners. Suddenly improvisations appeared. Substituting chicken for other meats became commonplace. For instance, many restaurants came up with recipes for chili made with turkey or chicken.

Restaurants were the first to introduce "free-range" chickens, raised with natural feed. Now a preponderance of upscale restaurants prefers cooking with free-range chickens. It didn't take long for the public marketplace to follow suit.

Restaurateurs also encouraged duck farmers across the nation to produce broad-breasted Muscovy ducks and to market only the breasts for convenience.

With the growth of ethnic populations in the United States, restaurant fare began reflecting a changed palate, and the column started receiving requests for Jerk Chicken from Jamaican restaurants, Tostaditas from Mexican restaurants and Orange Chicken from Chinese chain restaurants.

Here is a representative grouping of poultry recipes that give an idea of what "Culinary SOS" readers enjoy most.

White Lightning Chili ◆ Marston's

Chicken Dijon ◆ The Egg & The Eye

Chicken Marsala ◆ Papalucci's Italian Restaurant

Chicken Piccata ◆ Revere House

Poulet Rôti Fermière ◆ Taix French Restaurant

Chicken Tostadita ◆ El Cholo

Orange Chicken ◆ Panda Express

Stir-Fried Spicy Chicken ◆ ZenZero

Chicken Chilaquiles ◆ Border Grill

Jerk Chicken ◆ Cha Cha Cha Encino

Pollo alla Cacciatori ◆ Ristorante Cacciatori

Roasted Wild Turkey with Cornbread-Bacon Stuffing ◆ Windows on the World

Vinegar Turkey Breasts ◆ Border Grill

Turkey Patties (Polpettine Misteriose) ◆ Sostanza

WHITE LIGHTNING CHILI
Marston's, Pasadena

In the 1980s chicken became the favored meat for health reasons, and restaurants everywhere introduced "white chili," made with white beans and chicken. Marston's version was one of the best.

1 pound dried small white beans
2 large onions, chopped
3 cloves garlic, minced
Pinch of ground cloves
1 tablespoon ground cumin
2 teaspoons dried oregano
1 can (8 to 9 ounces) diced green chiles
1 or 2 jalapeños, minced
5 to 6 cups chicken broth
10 boneless chicken breast halves
Shredded Monterey Jack cheese (optional)
Guacamole (optional)

Combine beans, onions, garlic, cloves, cumin, oregano, chiles and jalapeños in large saucepan and add enough broth to cover by 2 inches. Cook, adding stock or water as necessary to keep beans covered, until beans are tender, about 1 hour.

Grill or broil chicken breast halves until juices run clear when pierced with fork, about 5 to 7 minutes per side. Cool and dice chicken. Add to chili mixture and heat through. Garnish each serving with cheese and guacamole if desired.

◆◆◆

10 servings. Each serving, without cheese or guacamole, contains about: 241 calories; 400 mg sodium; 78 mg cholesterol; 12 grams fat; 4 grams carbohydrate; 28 grams protein; 0.3 gram fiber.

CHICKEN DIJON
The Egg & The Eye, Los Angeles

When readers request a recipe for chicken Dijon, we often reply with this version originally from The Egg & The Eye, once located across the street from the Los Angeles County Museum of Art.

4 boneless, skinless chicken breast halves
3 tablespoons butter or margarine
1/4 cup chopped onion
1/2 cup dry white wine
2 tablespoons Dijon mustard
1 1/2 cups whipping cream
Pinch of fresh or dried rosemary
Pinch of fresh or dried thyme
Pinch of fresh or dried tarragon
Salt, pepper

Flatten chicken breast halves into cutlets. Melt 2 tablespoons butter in large skillet. Add chicken and cook until golden on both sides. Remove and keep warm.

Melt remaining butter in same skillet. Add onion and sauté until tender. Add wine and mustard and simmer until mixture is reduced by half. Add whipping cream and simmer until sauce is thick enough to coat a metal spoon.

Strain sauce, then add rosemary, thyme and tarragon. Season to taste with salt and pepper. Pour sauce over chicken breasts and serve.

❖ *Chef's Tip*: Chicken breasts with bone in can be used in place of cutlets. After browning chicken pieces, cover and cook 25 to 30 minutes or until tender. Serve chicken pieces covered with sauce.

4 servings. Each serving contains about: 606 calories; 489 mg sodium; 244 mg cholesterol; 44 grams fat; 4 grams carbohydrate; 41 grams protein; 0.23 gram fiber.

CHICKEN MARSALA

Papalucci's Italian Restaurant, Long Beach

Use either sweet or dry Marsala, depending on your taste.

6 skinless, boneless chicken breast halves, about 4 ounces each
All-purpose flour
3 tablespoons olive oil
2 large onions, chopped
3 tablespoons chopped Italian parsley
8 ounces fresh mushrooms, sliced
Garlic salt
3/4 cup Marsala

Pound each chicken breast half between sheets of parchment or wax paper until 1/2 inch thick. Dip in flour to coat well.

Heat oil in large skillet. Fry chicken until browned, about 5 minutes per side. Remove from skillet and keep warm. Add onions, parsley and mushrooms to skillet and cook until softened, about 10 minutes. Return chicken to skillet and sprinkle with garlic salt to taste. Add Marsala and simmer until sauce is reduced and thickened, about 5 to 10 minutes. Serve immediately.

◆◆◆

6 servings. Each serving contains about: 234 calories; 127 mg sodium; 66 mg cholesterol; 8 grams fat; 9 grams carbohydrate; 28 grams protein; 0.54 gram fiber.

CHICKEN PICCATA
Revere House, Tustin

Many restaurants, such as Revere House, use chicken instead of veal to prepare the classic piccata.

1/2 cup all-purpose flour
Salt
White pepper
8 boneless chicken breast halves, about 7 ounces each
Butter
1 1/2 pounds mushrooms, sliced
1/4 cup capers
1 cup dry white wine
1/2 cup lemon juice
1 tablespoon chopped garlic
1 tablespoon chopped shallot

Combine flour, salt and white pepper. Dredge both sides of chicken breasts in flour mixture.

Heat 6 tablespoons butter in skillet over medium heat. Add chicken breasts and cook until golden brown, about 10 minutes per side. Add mushrooms and capers and sauté briefly. Set aside and keep warm.

Bring wine, lemon juice, garlic and shallot to boil in saucepan. Simmer until reduced by half. Remove from heat and add 1/2 cup (1 stick) butter, 1 tablespoon at a time, stirring until melted after each addition. Pour sauce over chicken breasts and serve.

◆◆◆

8 servings. Each serving contains about: 407 calories; 426 mg sodium; 118 mg cholesterol; 23 grams fat; 12 grams carbohydrate; 34 grams protein; 0.68 gram fiber.

POULET RÔTI FERMIÈRE

Taix French Restaurant, Los Angeles

Readers who have frequented Les Frères Taix (renamed Taix French Restaurant) for the last several decades say the smell of its roast chicken and Bordelaise sauce is reminiscent of a cozy Parisian side-street bistro.

CHICKEN:

2 whole chickens, about 2 to 2 1/4 pounds each

Salt, pepper

1/2 cup canola oil

BORDELAISE GRAVY:

2 cups beef or chicken broth

1/4 cup reserved chicken drippings (optional)

I small bay leaf

1/2 teaspoon crushed dried oregano

1/2 teaspoon crushed dried thyme

1/2 teaspoon crushed dried rosemary

3/4 teaspoon sugar

I 1/2 teaspoons tomato paste

I 1/2 teaspoons caramel coloring or beef glaze

2 tablespoons cornstarch

1/2 cup dry red wine

CHICKEN:

Preheat oven to 425 degrees. Rinse chickens, pat dry and truss. Season to taste with salt and pepper. Pour oil into bottom of roasting pan and heat in oven until very hot. Add chickens, breast side up. Roast 30 minutes.

Turn chickens breast side down and roast 30 minutes longer or until nicely browned. Remove chickens from oven and reserve drippings for gravy, if desired. Carve chickens and serve with Bordelaise Gravy.

BORDELAISE GRAVY:

Place broth in saucepan. Skim fat from chicken drippings and add to broth if desired. Add bay leaf, oregano, thyme, rosemary, sugar, tomato paste and caramel coloring and bring to slow boil, stirring constantly.

Mix cornstarch and wine and slowly add to stock mixture, stirring constantly until sauce is thickened and shiny. Reduce heat and simmer 2 minutes. Makes about 2 1/2 cups.

◆◆◆

4 servings. Each serving contains about: 930 calories; 1,079 mg sodium; 218 mg cholesterol; 72 grams fat; 9 grams carbohydrate; 59 grams protein; 0.29 gram fiber.

CHICKEN TOSTADITA

El Cholo, La Habra

For many years, El Cholo has graciously provided this and many other recipes to "Culinary SOS" readers.

CHICKEN:

4 medium chicken breast halves

1/2 cup lime juice

Salt, pepper

2 cups shredded iceberg lettuce

I small head butter lettuce, shredded

1/2 cup shredded red cabbage

1/4 cup thinly sliced green beans

1/4 cup green peas

1/2 cup julienned cooked or canned beets

1/2 small jicama, peeled and julienned

1/4 cup sliced pitted ripe olives

I avocado, peeled and sliced

4 ounces aged dry Monterey Jack cheese, shredded

1/2 cup sour cream

1/4 cup shortening or lard

6 10-inch wholewheat flour tortillas

ORANGE-LIME DRESSING:

1/2 cup orange juice

2 tablespoons lime juice

3 tablespoons olive oil

I 1/2 teaspoons Dijon mustard

2 tablespoons cider vinegar

2 tablespoons rice vinegar

2 tablespoons mixed chopped fresh basil, cilantro, marjoram and oregano

1/2 teaspoon pepper

I 1/2 teaspoons sugar

Salt

CHICKEN:

Marinate chicken breast halves in lime juice at least 2 hours or overnight. Season to taste with salt and pepper. Grill until browned on both sides. Cool, then cut into strips.

Combine lettuces, cabbage, green beans, peas, beets, jicama, olives, avocado, cheese and 1/4 cup sour cream. Toss with enough Orange-Lime Dressing to moisten. Set aside.

Heat shortening in skillet over medium-high heat. Add tortillas one at a time and fry until spotted with brown, about 1 minute per side. Drain on paper towels.

Place 1 tortilla on each of six plates. Divide salad among tortillas. Top with grilled chicken strips and remaining sour cream. Serve with remaining Orange-Lime Dressing.

ORANGE-LIME DRESSING:

Combine orange and lime juices, olive oil, mustard, vinegars, herbs, pepper and sugar. Season to taste with salt and mix well. Cover and chill until serving time. Makes about 1 1/4 cups.

◆◆◆

6 servings. Each serving contains about: 718 calories; 643 mg sodium; 86 mg cholesterol; 50 grams fat; 38 grams carbohydrate; 30 grams protein; 2.4 grams fiber.

ORANGE CHICKEN
Panda Express Restaurants

In lieu of dried orange peel, this basic dish can be prepared with other flavorings, such as dried lemon or candied ginger. If you don't have dried orange peel, add the grated zest of one orange to the sauce for flavor.

CHICKEN:
2 pounds boneless chicken pieces, skinned
1 egg
1 1/2 teaspoons salt
White pepper
Vegetable or peanut oil
1/4 cup all-purpose flour
1/2 cup plus 1 tablespoon cornstarch
1 tablespoon minced fresh ginger
1 teaspoon minced garlic
Pinch of crushed hot red chiles
2 to 4 pieces dried orange peel
1/4 cup chopped green onions
1 tablespoon rice wine
1/4 cup water
1/2 to 1 teaspoon sesame oil

ORANGE CHICKEN SAUCE:
1 1/2 tablespoons soy sauce
1 1/2 tablespoons water
5 tablespoons sugar
5 tablespoons distilled white vinegar

CHICKEN:
Cut chicken pieces into 2-inch squares and place in large bowl. Stir in egg, salt, pepper and 1 tablespoon oil and mix well. Mix flour and 1/2 cup cornstarch. Add chicken pieces and toss to coat.

Heat oil for deep frying in wok or deep fryer to 375 degrees. Add chicken pieces in batches and fry 3 to 4 minutes or until golden and crisp; do not overcook or chicken will be tough. Remove chicken from oil with slotted spoon and drain on paper towels. Set aside.

Clean wok and heat 15 seconds over high heat. Add I tablespoon oil. Add ginger and garlic and stir-fry until fragrant. Add chiles, orange peel and green onions and stir-fry briefly. Add rice wine and stir 3 seconds. Discard orange peel. Add Orange Chicken Sauce and bring to boil. Add cooked chicken, stirring until well mixed. Stir water into remaining I tablespoon cornstarch until smooth.

Add cornstarch mixture to chicken and heat until sauce is thickened. Stir in sesame oil. Serve at once.

ORANGE CHICKEN SAUCE:

Mix soy sauce, water, sugar and vinegar. Makes about I cup.

◆◆◆

6 servings. Each serving contains about: 357 calories; 941 mg sodium; 115 mg cholesterol; 16 grams fat; 27 grams carbohydrate; 26 grams protein; 0.09 gram fiber.

STIR-FRIED SPICY CHICKEN

ZenZero, Santa Monica

We're so glad ZenZero's Daniel Flores shared this recipe. Now it's a staple on many of our readers' menus.

CHICKEN:
I carrot, diced
I parsnip, diced
1/4 cup Asian long beans or green beans, diced
12 ounces ground chicken
2 cloves garlic, minced
I teaspoon Asian sesame oil
I tablespoon peanut oil
I tablespoon molasses
1 1/2 teaspoons soy sauce
Salt, pepper
6 radicchio leaves
6 Boston lettuce leaves
I carrot, finely julienned
1/4 small cantaloupe, peeled and julienned
1/4 cup sugar-coated peanuts

PEANUT SAUCE:
1/2 cup creamy peanut butter
3 ounces canned sweetened cream of coconut
1/4 cup soy sauce
2 tablespoons lemon juice

CHICKEN:
Briefly cook diced carrot in lightly salted, rapidly boiling water. When carrot turns bright orange (about 3 to 5 minutes), remove immediately with slotted spoon and place in ice water to chill. Repeat with parsnip and long beans.

Season chicken with garlic and sesame oil. Heat peanut oil in wok. Add ground chicken mixture and brown without stirring. Drain vegetables and pat dry. When chicken is brown, add cooked carrot, parsnip and long beans and stir-fry briefly. Add molasses, soy sauce, and salt and pepper to taste.

Arrange radicchio and Boston lettuce leaves around outside of platter, leaving center open. Place chicken over greens. Fill center with small dishes containing raw carrot, cantaloupe, peanuts and Peanut Sauce.

PEANUT SAUCE:
Stir together peanut butter, cream of coconut, soy sauce and lemon juice until smooth. Hold at room temperature. Makes about 1 1/4 cups.

◆◆◆

4 servings. Each serving with peanut sauce, contains about: 499 calories; 1,451 mg sodium; 60 mg cholesterol; 32 grams fat; 26 grams carbohydrate; 32 grams protein; 5.47 grams fiber.

CHICKEN CHILAQUILES

Border Grill, Santa Monica

You can make panfuls of this dish relatively inexpensively. Serve leftover Tomatillo Salsa as a dip or as a condiment alongside Mexican dishes.

CHICKEN:
Vegetable oil
12 day-old corn tortillas
8 chicken breast halves
Chicken broth or water
Salt, pepper
1 cup thinly sliced onion
2 cups shredded Monterey Jack cheese
2 cups shredded Cheddar cheese

TOMATILLO SALSA:
2 pounds tomatillos
1 large onion, quartered
5 jalapeños
2 bunches cilantro, stemmed
Salt, pepper

CHILAQUILES SAUCE:
3 cups Tomatillo Salsa
1 cup whipping cream
Salt, pepper

CHICKEN:
In 1/2 cup oil, lightly fry tortillas one at a time until soft, not crisp, adding more oil as needed. Set aside.

Place chicken breast halves in large skillet. Add chicken broth to cover and season to taste with salt and pepper. Cover and poach over medium heat until chicken is tender, about 20 minutes. Drain chicken and cool. Remove skin and bones from chicken. Cut meat into 1-inch pieces. Set aside.

Dip each tortilla in Chilaquiles Sauce to coat well; set aside. Mix onion and 1/3 of Chilaquiles Sauce. Mix chicken breast pieces with some of Chilaquiles Sauce. Mix cheeses.

Again dip tortillas in remaining Chilaquiles Sauce. Turn to coat well.

Preheat oven to 350 degrees. Arrange 1/3 of tortillas in bottom of generously buttered 4-quart rectangular baking dish. Top with half of onion mixture, half of chicken mixture and half of cheese mixture. Cover with another 1/3 of tortillas. Layer with remaining ingredients, ending with remaining sauced tortillas on top. Press firmly to mold chilaquiles into dish. Spoon remaining sauce over as desired, reserving any leftover sauce for another use. Cover with foil, but do not let foil touch top layer of chilaquiles. Bake 45 to 50 minutes or until heated through.

❖ *Chef's Tip*: To make in individual servings, layer tortillas (cut up if needed), onion mixture, chicken breast mixture and cheese mixture in eight buttered ovenproof soup bowls. Cover with foil and bake at 300 degrees 40 minutes.

TOMATILLO SALSA:

Process tomatillos, onions, jalapeños and cilantro in food processor until large chunks have disappeared. Transfer to blender and blend until smooth. Season to taste with salt and pepper. Makes about 4 3/4 cups.

CHILAQUILES SAUCE:

Combine Tomatillo Salsa, whipping cream and salt and pepper to taste. Mix well. Makes I quart.

◆◆◆

8 servings. Each serving contains about: 742 calories; 749 mg sodium; 203 mg cholesterol; 41 grams fat; 34 grams carbohydrate; 62 grams protein; 3.37 grams fiber.

JERK CHICKEN
Cha Cha Cha, Encino

A good suggestion from Cha Cha Cha: Read the instructions carefully before you begin preparing this twice-cooked chicken dish.

2 cups pineapple juice
2 cups orange juice
1 cup Worcestershire sauce
2 tablespoons minced garlic
1 ½ tablespoons dried thyme
4 teaspoons chili powder
4 teaspoons red pepper flakes, or to taste
1 tablespoon salt
1 tablespoon black pepper
1 tablespoon dried oregano
1 teaspoon ground coriander
1 teaspoon curry powder
1 teaspoon garlic powder
1 teaspoon ground ginger
1 teaspoon turmeric
½ teaspoon cayenne pepper
¼ teaspoon ground allspice
6 to 8 boneless chicken breast halves

In bowl large enough to hold marinade and chicken pieces, combine all ingredients except chicken and mix well. Add chicken breasts, turning to coat well. Cover and marinate in refrigerator 24 hours.

Remove chicken and reserve marinade. Grill chicken over medium heat until partially cooked, about 4 minutes per side. Let cool a few minutes, then cut each breast in half. Brush with more marinade, then grill over low heat until chicken is done, 4 to 5 minutes, brushing frequently with marinade to keep moist.

6 servings. Each serving contains about: 309 calories; 584 mg sodium; 109 mg cholesterol; 16 grams fat; 3 grams carbohydrate; 36 grams protein; 0.58 gram fiber.

POLLO alla CACCIATORI

Ristorante Cacciatori, Cartosio, Acqui Terme, Italy

Restaurant recipe requests come to us in many forms. In this case, the reader hadn't even tasted the chicken cacciatore recipe she requested. She had read an article written by Times restaurant critic S. I. Virbila, who simply described the dish after trying it at a restaurant in the Piedmont province of Italy. Virbila was kind enough to obtain the recipe for us.

2 tablespoons olive oil
1 chicken (about 3 1/2 pounds), cut into 12 pieces
1 4-inch rosemary branch
2 plum tomatoes, peeled and chopped, or 3 canned Italian plum tomatoes, coarsely chopped
1/2 onion, sliced
Pinch of nutmeg
1/2 cup dry white wine
Salt, pepper

Heat olive oil in skillet over medium-high heat. Add chicken and sauté until golden on both sides, about 5 minutes per side. Add rosemary, tomatoes, onion, nutmeg and wine. Season with salt and pepper to taste.

Cover and cook over medium-high heat until chicken is tender and juices run clear when chicken is pricked with fork, about 50 minutes. If sauce is too liquid, cook uncovered a few minutes longer. Serve chicken with tomatoes and pan juices.

◆◆◆

6 servings. Each serving contains about: 384 calories; 157 mg sodium; 112 mg cholesterol; 27 grams fat; 3 grams carbohydrate; 28 grams protein; 0.25 gram fiber.

ROASTED WILD TURKEY
with CORNBREAD-BACON DRESSING
Windows on the World, World Trade Center, New York City

You don't need a wild turkey to make this dish. Use any good brand.

CORNBREAD-BACON DRESSING
3 cups crumbled homemade or store-bought cornbread
1 cup cubed sourdough bread
1/2 cup buttermilk
1/4 cup molasses
1 cup chicken broth
3 eggs, beaten
8 ounces smoked slab bacon, cut into 1/2-inch cubes
1 cup chopped green onions
2 fresh jalapeños, seeded and finely chopped
3 tablespoons ancho chile powder
1/2 cup chopped pecans
Salt, pepper

TURKEY:
1 turkey, 12 to 14 pounds
Salt, pepper
2 to 3 bay leaves
1 head unpeeled garlic, split in half
1 onion, diced
1 cup hot water, plus more as needed
3 tablespoons salted butter, melted

CORNBREAD-BACON DRESSING:
   Combine cornbread, sourdough bread, buttermilk, molasses, chicken broth and eggs in bowl and refrigerate 3 to 8 hours.
   Place bacon in heated skillet and cook until browned. Pour off and reserve fat.
   Add green onions and jalapeños to bacon and cook 5 minutes. Let cool.
   Preheat oven to 350 degrees. Grease 3-quart casserole. Add soaked bread, chile powder and pecans to green onion mixture. Season with salt and pepper to taste. Spoon into prepared casserole and drizzle top with several tablespoons reserved

bacon drippings.

Bake dressing until top is browned and crisp, about 30 to 35 minutes. Let cool 15 minutes before serving.

TURKEY:

Preheat oven to 425 degrees. Season turkey inside and out with salt and pepper. Place bay leaves, garlic and onion inside cavity. Set turkey breast side down on rack in roasting pan. Pour water into pan and roast 30 minutes.

Turn turkey breast side up and brush with melted butter. Reduce heat to 350 degrees and roast turkey until juices run clear when thigh joint is pierced with fork and when meat thermometer inserted in thickest part of thigh registers 165 degrees, 1 to 1 1/2 hours, adding more water to pan as needed.

Remove turkey from oven and let stand 20 minutes before carving. Serve with Cornbread-Bacon Dressing.

◆◆◆

8 servings. Each serving, with stuffing, contains about: 1,105 calories; 990 mg sodium; 420 mg cholesterol; 61 grams fat; 34 grams carbohydrate; 99 grams protein; 1.22 grams fiber.

❖ *Chef's Tip*: If your oven is large enough to accommodate both turkey and dressing, add the casserole of dressing to the oven about one hour after the turkey goes in, and both should be ready at about the same time. If your oven will accommodate only a turkey, cook the dressing before you roast the bird, then reheat the dressing for 15 to 20 minutes in a 350-degree oven while the meat rests and you prepare whatever gravy you want to serve.

VINEGAR TURKEY BREASTS

Border Grill, Santa Monica

Readers love this new way of serving turkey.

TURKEY:
2 1/4 pounds boneless turkey breast, cut into thin scallops
Salt, pepper
Olive oil
7 1/2 tablespoons chilled unsalted butter
2 medium-size red onions, diced
1 cup white wine vinegar
2 cups turkey or chicken broth
1 tablespoon freshly cracked black pepper

SEARED GREENS:
3 bunches mustard greens or red or green chard
4 tablespoons unsalted butter
3/4 teaspoon salt
1/2 teaspoon freshly ground black pepper

TURKEY:
Cover turkey slices with plastic wrap and pound to flatten. Sprinkle with salt and pepper. Brush lightly with olive oil. Set aside.

Melt 3 tablespoons butter in medium skillet over low heat. Add onions, season with salt and sauté, tossing and shaking pan frequently, until onions are golden, about 15 minutes. Add vinegar. Raise heat to high and boil until liquid is reduced by half. Add turkey broth and reduce by half again.

Thinly slice remaining cold butter. Reduce heat to low and gradually whisk butter into sauce. Remove from heat and stir in cracked pepper.

Grill turkey slices less than 1 minute per side, or sauté in hot skillet with additional butter or olive oil until golden on both sides; do not overcook. Serve over bed of Seared Greens with sauce drizzled over.

SEARED GREENS:

Trim and discard stems of greens. Wash and dry leaves. Stack leaves, roll up and cut across roll into 1-inch strips.

Melt 1 tablespoon butter in large skillet over medium-high heat until bubbly. Sauté 1/4 of greens with 1/4 of salt and pepper until greens are limp, about 30 to 60 seconds. If greens begin to color before they wilt, sprinkle with a few drops of water to create steam. Transfer to platter and repeat procedure with remaining 3 batches.

◆◆◆

6 servings. Each serving, with greens, contains about: 447 calories; 843 mg sodium; 149 mg cholesterol; 29 grams fat; 12 grams carbohydrate; 37 grams protein; 1.48 grams fiber.

TURKEY PATTIES (Polpettine Misteriose)

Sostanza, West Los Angeles

As well as making wonderful picnic burgers, these patties are fine as hors d'oeuvres if prepared bite-size.

TURKEY:
8 ounces coarse-textured bread, thinly sliced
1/2 cup milk
1 2/3 pounds ground turkey
2 cloves garlic, minced
1/4 teaspoon nutmeg
Salt
White pepper
All-purpose flour
1/4 cup olive oil

ONION MARMALADE:
1/4 cup extra-virgin olive oil
4 medium onions, thinly sliced
1/4 cup balsamic vinegar
1/2 cup white wine
2 tablespoons chopped Italian parsley
1/2 cup chicken broth

TURKEY:
Soak bread in milk until soft. Squeeze out bread and discard extra liquid.

Place ground turkey in bowl and mix with soaked bread, garlic and nutmeg. Add salt and white pepper to taste and mix well, about 5 minutes.

Form mixture into 6 uniform balls, flattening slightly between palms of hands. Place on wax paper. Dust with flour.

Heat oil in skillet over medium heat and fry patties until browned on both sides. Remove and keep warm. Discard excess oil. Add Onion Marmalade to skillet and cook over medium heat until thickened. Return patties to skillet and heat through. Serve immediately.

ONION MARMALADE:

Heat olive oil in skillet over medium heat. Add onions, cover, reduce heat and cook until onions begin to caramelize, about 20 minutes, stirring every few minutes.

Add vinegar and wine and cook until liquid is absorbed. Add parsley and chicken broth, increase heat to high and cook to semi-thick consistency, about 15 to 20 minutes. Makes about I cup.

◆◆◆

6 servings. Each serving contains about: 363 calories; 269 mg sodium; 59 mg cholesterol; 12 grams fat; 32 grams carbohydrate; 28 grams protein; 3.45 grams fiber.

MEAT

◆◆◆

This chapter contains nearly all of the best meat recipes that have appeared in the "Culinary SOS" column. If it's not here, you'll probably find what you're looking for in the companion "Dear SOS: 30 Years of Recipe Requests" cookbook, published previously by The Times.

If you've ever wondered how Lawry's Prime Rib cooks its signature cut to perfection, you'll find the recipe here, with temperatures and roasting times to help you. If you hunger for the Brandied Short Ribs from The Grill, that recipe, too, is in this chapter. So are the recipes for the Bistro Garden's famous pot roast and Santa Anita racetrack's incomparable corned beef. They're top reader favorites.

Even though people talk about eating more fish and chicken, steak is No. I when it comes to meat requests. So in this chapter you'll find the top favorites that'll make your mouth water: Whiskey-Marinated Rib Eye Steaks from a Laughlin casino restaurant; Steak Fajitas from Chili's; Poor Man's Pepper Steak from the Dal Rae Restaurant; and, of course, skirt steak from the Daily Grill, the most popular meat item on their menu. We've also included an Italian specialty that's relatively new on the restaurant scene — Bistecca, a Florentine steak cooked so that the juices are sealed in, from Silvio di Mori, who now owns Mimosa.

Chili is a favorite of many of our readers. There is a typical Midwestern type here — you heap it on spaghetti and hot dogs — from Skyline Chili, one of the oldest chili parlors in Cincinnati.

Veal, although no longer the most popular meat around, still has fans. Classic Osso Buco and Veal Marsala are among readers' favorites. Enjoy.

Pot Roast ◆ Bistro Garden at Coldwater

Prime Rib ◆ Lawry's Prime Rib

Brandied Short Ribs ◆ The Grill

Corned Beef ◆ Santa Anita

Meatloaf ◆ Daily Grill

Bistecca ◆ Tutto Bene

Skirt Steak ◆ Daily Grill

Whiskey-Marinated Rib Eye Steaks ◆ Colorado Belle Casino

Gaucho Steaks with Chimichurri Vinaigrette ◆ Ciudad

Steak Marinade and Fajitas ◆ Chili's Restaurants

Tangerine Beef ◆ China Panda

Flank Steak ◆ Mandarette

Skyline Chili ◆ Skyline Chili

Poor Man's Pepper Steak ◆ Dal Rae

Lamb Shanks ◆ Musso & Frank Grill

Indonesian Rack of Lamb ◆ Trader Vic's

Pork Chops with Tomato Sauce ◆ Il Gazebo

Veal Marsala ◆ Mario's Cooking for Friends

Osso Buco ◆ Mi Piace

POT ROAST
The Bistro Garden at Coldwater, Studio City

The Bistro Garden still serves pot roast as a Wednesday special, and Harry Klibigat, an executive chef at both the original Bistro Garden and the Studio City branch, still prepares it. It comes with potato pancakes. Luscious!

POT ROAST:
2 1/2 pounds tri-tip or chuck roast, trimmed of fat
Salt, pepper
1/4 cup canola oil
I medium-size white onion, chopped
2 carrots, chopped
2 stalks celery, chopped
2 cloves garlic, minced
Pinch of sugar
Pinch of dried rosemary or thyme
1/4 cup tomato puree
2 cups dry red wine
1/2 cup all-purpose flour
I tablespoon butter

POTATO PANCAKES:
3 large russet potatoes, peeled, grated and partially drained
1/2 medium onion, finely chopped
I bunch chives, thinly sliced
2 eggs
1/3 cup all-purpose flour
Salt, pepper
Canola oil for frying

POT ROAST:
   Season beef with salt and pepper. Heat oil in roasting pan and sear beef until even-ly browned on all sides, about 15 minutes. Remove from pan and keep warm.
   To the pot add onion, carrots, celery, garlic, sugar and rosemary. Sauté until onion is browned, about 15 minutes. Add tomato puree and sauté several seconds. Add

wine and simmer over medium-high heat until reduced by half, about 20 minutes. Add flour to sauce, stirring until smooth. Simmer a few minutes.

Preheat oven to 350 degrees. Add beef to sauce and bring to boil. Cover and braise beef in oven 1 1/2 to 2 hours or until meat is fork tender. Remove beef and keep warm. Skim off fat and strain sauce. Simmer sauce to thicken and reduce slightly. Adjust seasoning. Swirl in butter and mix well. Serve with Potato Pancakes.

POTATO PANCAKES:

Combine potatoes, onion, chives, eggs, flour and salt and pepper to taste in large bowl. Mix well.

Pour oil into skillet to depth of 1/2 inch; heat. Using about 1/4 cup potato mixture for each pancake, add to hot oil and flatten. Fry until golden brown on one side, then turn to cook on other side. Drain pancakes on paper towels. Continue to cook pancakes, using more oil as needed, until batter is used. Serve with pot roast.

6 servings. Each serving, with 2 pancakes, contains about: 869 calories; 337 mg sodium; 172 mg cholesterol; 26 grams fat; 116 grams carbohydrate; 47 grams protein; 11.52 grams fiber.

PRIME RIB

Lawry's Prime Rib, Los Angeles

Who can deny that Lawry's Prime Rib serves some of the best prime rib known to man? Well, we have the recipe, thanks to the generosity of the Lawry's people. We pass on a few bits of advice for cooking this excellent beef.

I prime rib, 8 to 10 pounds
Rock salt
Seasoned salt

Preheat oven to 325 degrees. Place prime rib fat side up in baking pan. Rub with rock salt, then with seasoned salt.

Roast until meat thermometer registers I30 degrees for rare (about I8 to 20 minutes per pound), I40 degrees for medium rare (22 minutes per pound), I50 degrees for medium (25 minutes per pound), or I60 degrees for well done (27 minutes per pound).

Let roast stand 20 minutes before carving. To carve, place beef on its side and cut across grain toward ribs.

◆◆◆

10 servings. Each serving contains about: 561 calories; 904 mg sodium; I61 mg cholesterol; 37 grams fat; 0 carbohydrate; 54 grams protein; 0 fiber.

❖ *Chef's Tip*: Lawry's prime rib is huge, more than I5 pounds. We reduced the roast to home size and also cut the cooking time. However, the roasting method is the same. We strongly urge you to use a meat thermometer for determining doneness because cooking time alone is not always an accurate indicator. Lawry's prefers to cook its beef rare. Be sure to insert the meat thermometer into the center of the roast for the most accurate reading.

BRANDIED SHORT RIBS

The Grill, Beverly Hills

Where do you find kosher-cut ribs? Most butchers will cut them for you. If not, use regular short ribs.

6 tablespoons vegetable oil
2 1/2 pounds kosher-cut short ribs
I cup diced mixed onion, celery and carrot
I bay leaf
1/4 cup brandy
2 cups beef broth
I tablespoon arrowroot
Salt, pepper
I onion, cut into 3-inch julienne
I turnip, peeled and cut into 3-inch julienne
Chopped fresh parsley

Heat 2 tablespoons oil in large skillet. Add short ribs and sauté until well browned, about 2 minutes on each side. Remove from pan and set aside.

Preheat oven to 450 degrees. Add 2 tablespoons oil to skillet and heat. Add diced onion, celery, carrot and bay leaf and sauté until browned, 5 minutes. Place vegetables and short ribs in roasting pan and braise in oven 15 to 20 minutes. Add brandy and beef broth, reduce oven heat to 350 degrees and bake, covered, until meat falls away from bone, I 3/4 to 2 hours. Remove short ribs from pan and set aside. Discard vegetables.

Strain pan juices. Heat I tablespoon oil in small skillet. Stir in arrowroot until smooth paste forms. Stir a small amount of pan juices into arrowroot paste, then return mixture to remaining pan juices and mix well. Strain again. Season to taste with salt and pepper.

Heat remaining tablespoon oil. Add julienned onion and turnip and sauté until lightly browned. Place vegetables on top of short ribs. Pour sauce over vegetables. Sprinkle with parsley.

4 servings. Each serving contains about: 365 calories; 865 mg sodium; 88 mg cholesterol; 22 grams fat; 9 grams carbohydrate; 30 grams protein; 1.63 grams fiber.

CORNED BEEF

Santa Anita racetrack, Arcadia

We can't imagine any "Dear SOS" cookbook without this all-time favorite.

CORNED BEEF:

1 corned beef brisket, 5 to 6 pounds
3 tablespoons pickling spice
Prepared mustard
Mixed fruit jelly
Sesame seeds
Sauce Remoulade (optional)

SAUCE REMOULADE:

2 tablespoons lemon juice
2 tablespoons tarragon vinegar
2 tablespoons Dijon or other French-style mustard
2 tablespoons prepared horseradish
1 tablespoon chopped fresh parsley
1 teaspoon paprika
$^{1}/_{4}$ teaspoon cayenne pepper
1 cup vegetable oil
$^{1}/_{4}$ cup finely chopped celery
$^{1}/_{4}$ cup finely chopped green onions
1 tablespoon minced capers

CORNED BEEF:

Place brisket in boiling water to cover. Add pickling spice and simmer until tender, about 3 $^{1}/_{2}$ to 4 hours. Do not overcook.

Remove brisket from pot and let stand 15 minutes. Preheat oven to 375 degrees. Place brisket in baking pan and cover surface lightly with mustard. Let stand 10 minutes. Spread jelly over brisket and sprinkle with sesame seeds. Bake until set, 15 to 20 minutes. Serve with Sauce Remoulade if desired.

SAUCE REMOULADE:

Mix lemon juice, vinegar, mustard, horseradish, parsley, paprika and cayenne. Beat in oil, then add celery, green onions and capers. Makes about 2 $^{1}/_{2}$ cups.

◆◆◆

8 servings. Each serving, without sauce, contains about: 381 calories; 168 mg sodium; 132 mg cholesterol; 18 grams fat; 5 grams carbohydrate; 46 grams protein; 1.09 grams fiber.

MEATLOAF
Daily Grill, Brentwood

Readers travel far and wide for a taste of the Daily Grill Meatloaf. You'll find the seasonings interesting. You can double the recipe, cut it in half or make individual loaves to freeze for use anytime.

1 1/2 teaspoons olive oil
1 clove garlic, minced
1/2 teaspoon minced shallot
1/2 cup diced onion
1/2 cup diced celery
1/2 cup diced carrot
2 pounds ground chuck
2 eggs
1 cup sourdough bread crumbs
2 tablespoons tomato puree
1 teaspoon salt
1/4 teaspoon black pepper
2 tablespoons Dijon mustard
1/8 teaspoon ground fennel seeds
1/2 teaspoon paprika
1/2 teaspoon Worcestershire sauce

Heat olive oil in skillet over medium-high heat. Add garlic and shallot and sauté until tender. Add onion, celery and carrot and sauté 3 minutes. Let cool.

Preheat oven to 350 degrees. In bowl mix vegetables with meat, eggs, bread crumbs, tomato puree, salt, pepper, mustard, fennel, paprika and Worcestershire sauce. Pack into 8- or 9-inch loaf pan and bake until firm to touch, about 1 hour.

◆◆◆

6 servings. Each serving contains about: 294 calories; 677 mg sodium; 162 mg cholesterol; 10 grams fat; 12 grams carbohydrate; 36 grams protein; 0.4 gram fiber.

BISTECCA
Tutto Bene, Los Angeles

This recipe looks so simple you may think we're kidding. But only by trying this traditional Florentine method of cooking steak will you know the difference between steak and bistecca, the steak enjoyed by Italians.

2 pounds aged Porterhouse steak
Salt
Extra-virgin olive oil
Freshly ground pepper

Let steak stand at cool room temperature 4 hours before cooking. Broil without seasoning 6 to 8 minutes on one side. Add salt to taste on cooked side and turn with spatula (do not use fork). Broil 6 to 8 minutes more.

Add salt to taste on other side. Place steak on serving plate and cut slices off bone. Drizzle olive oil over slices. Season to taste with pepper.

◆◆◆

2 servings. Each serving contains about: 857 calories; 428 mg sodium; 188 mg cholesterol; 73 grams fat; 0 carbohydrate; 48 grams protein; 0 fiber.

❖ *Chef's Tip*: If you make sure not to puncture the meat when turning it, you'll lock in the juices and have a tender, juicy steak. Salt is another key element in keeping the meat moist and flavorful. It's especially important to use extra-virgin olive oil for taste enhancement.

SKIRT STEAK
Daily Grill, Los Angeles

Skirt steak, a relatively inexpensive cut, turns glamorous here. Keep the marinade in mind for other chewy meat cuts you want to tenderize (Tri-tip, rump and pork come to mind.) Game and game birds are also good candidates for fruit juice-based marinades.

6 skirt steaks, (about 6 ounces each), trimmed of fat
1/4 cup canola oil
1/2 cup light soy sauce
1/2 cup rice vinegar
1/4 cup orange juice
1/2 cup pineapple juice
I medium onion, coarsely chopped
1/4 cup English mustard

Place skirt steaks in nonaluminum pan in single layer. Combine oil, soy sauce, vinegar, orange juice, pineapple juice, onion and mustard. Pour mixture over steaks. Cover and marinate in refrigerator 12 to 24 hours.

Remove steaks from marinade and cook over medium-low coals or under broiler 4 inches from heat source to desired doneness, preferably medium rare, as overcooking may toughen steak.

◆◆◆

6 servings. Each serving contains about: 277 calories; 413 mg sodium; 64 mg cholesterol; 15 grams fat; 6 grams carbohydrate; 28 grams protein; 0.92 gram fiber.

WHISKEY-MARINATED RIB EYE STEAKS

Colorado Belle Casino, Laughlin, Nevada

When this recipe was tried in the Times test kitchen, we felt that the steaks were just as good without the gravy. But try it if you like. The chef uses Black Angus rib eye steak at the restaurant, but any tender steak is fine. Any whiskey or bourbon is fine, too.

STEAKS:
6 rib eye steaks
1/4 cup olive oil
2 to 3 cloves garlic, minced
1 tablespoon chopped fresh thyme
1 tablespoon chopped fresh rosemary
Salt
Freshly ground black pepper
Whiskey

GRAVY:
2 tablespoons olive oil
1 tablespoon minced red onion
1 teaspoon freshly ground black pepper
1 tablespoon minced garlic
1 tablespoon minced mixed fresh herbs, such as thyme, rosemary and parsley
3/4 cup whiskey
3 cups beef broth
1/4 cup cornstarch

STEAKS:
Place rib eye steaks in single layer in shallow pan. Sprinkle both sides with olive oil, garlic, thyme, rosemary, salt and pepper. Add enough whiskey to cover steaks halfway. Marinate several hours or overnight in refrigerator, turning steaks halfway through.

When ready to cook, remove steaks from pan and shake off excess marinade. Broil 2 inches from heat source or grill over hot coals to desired doneness. Serve with gravy.

GRAVY:

Heat olive oil in medium saucepan. Add onion, pepper, garlic and herbs and cook, stirring often, until onion is soft. Add whiskey and heat. Ignite, being careful to keep hands, clothing and face away from flames. When flames die down, add beef broth and simmer 20 minutes.

Mix cornstarch with enough water to form thin paste. Add to simmering gravy, stirring constantly until gravy thickens slightly. Pour into gravy boat and serve with steaks.

◆◆◆

6 servings. Each serving, with 2 tablespoons gravy, contains about: 461 calories; 529 mg sodium; 80 mg cholesterol; 25 grams fat; 12 grams carbohydrate; 29 grams protein; 0.30 gram fiber.

GAUCHO STEAKS
with CHIMICHURRI VINAIGRETTE
Ciudad, Los Angeles

Ciudad serves this dish with traditional Argentine chimichurri, a hot and spicy vinaigrette sprinkled onto the meat or used as a dip. Look for Argentine steaks at specialty markets or use regular rib eye.

GAUCHO STEAKS:
8 jalapeños
Nonstick cooking spray
20 cloves garlic
4 rib eye steaks (about 15 ounces each), preferably Argentine
Sea salt
Freshly ground pepper

CHIMICHURRI VINAIGRETTE:
2 teaspoons chopped garlic
1/2 teaspoon dried red pepper flakes
1/4 cup red wine vinegar
1/2 cup olive oil
Sea salt
Freshly ground pepper
1/4 cup chopped parsley

GAUCHO STEAKS:
Using tongs, roast jalapeños over stovetop flame, rotating so chiles blacken evenly on all sides, 3 to 5 minutes. (Alternatively, place on pan under broiler and broil a few minutes on each side until blackened.) Place chiles in bowl and cover with plastic wrap. Let stand 10 minutes. When cool enough to handle, peel charred skin. Stem and seed chiles and slice into thin strips. Set aside.

Coat saucepan lightly with cooking spray and roast garlic over medium-high heat, stirring occasionally, until cloves are fragrant and have softened, about 10 minutes. When cool, cut into thin slices.

Lay steaks flat on work surface. Make 2 incisions in each steak parallel to work surface to create pockets. Stuff each with roasted chiles and roasted garlic, dividing evenly among steaks. Season generously with salt and pepper.

Grill steaks over medium-high heat to desired doneness, 5 to 10 minutes per side. Serve with Chimichurri Vinaigrette.

CHIMICHURRI VINAIGRETTE:

Mix garlic, red pepper flakes, vinegar, oil and salt and pepper to taste. Add parsley just before serving. Makes about 3/4 cup.

◆◆◆

4 servings. Each serving, with 2 tablespoons vinaigrette, contains about: 604 calories; 362 mg sodium; 188 mg cholesterol; 33 grams fat; 8 grams carbohydrate; 66 grams protein; 0.38 gram fiber.

STEAK MARINADE and FAJITAS

Chili's Restaurants

This marinade can be used to flavor steaks, chops or poultry.

STEAK MARINADE:
3 cups soy sauce
2/3 cup honey
1/4 cup Worcestershire sauce
2 teaspoons minced garlic
1 tablespoon ground ginger
1 quart water

FAJITAS:
1 flank, skirt or sirloin steak, about 2 pounds
1 red bell pepper, seeded and cut into thin strips
1 green bell pepper, seeded and cut into thin strips
1 onion, thinly sliced
Cilantro sprigs (optional)
Hot cooked rice (optional)
Tortillas (optional)

STEAK MARINADE:

Combine soy sauce, honey, Worcestershire sauce, garlic, ginger and water in bowl. Place in jars with tight-fitting lids and use as needed to marinate steaks, chops or poultry for grilling or making fajitas. Makes 7 1/2 cups.

FAJITAS:

Place steak in 13 x 9-inch glass baking dish and cover with marinade. Cover and marinate in refrigerator 4 hours or overnight.

Drain meat and slice into thin strips. Heat skillet and add drained meat, red and green bell peppers, onion and enough marinade (1 to 2 tablespoons) to keep mixture from sticking to skillet. Stir-fry just until meat is done as desired.

Garnish with cilantro. Serve with rice, if desired, or place about 1/2 cup mixture in center of 1 tortilla. Add any favorite salsa or toppings.

◆◆◆

4 servings. Each serving, without salsa and rice, contains about: 333 calories; 127 mg sodium; 85 mg cholesterol; 17 grams fat; 7 grams carbohydrate; 35 grams protein; 0.40 gram fiber.

TANGERINE BEEF

China Panda, Orange County

Here is a typical tangerine beef recipe that readers often request.

TANGERINE BEEF:
I pound flank steak or other lean beef
Salt, pepper
I egg, beaten
1/4 cup cornstarch
3 tablespoons vegetable or peanut oil
4 dried red or green hot peppers
2 tablespoons chopped green onion
5 small pieces dried tangerine or orange peel

SEASONING SAUCE:
I tablespoon sugar
3 tablespoons soy sauce
I tablespoon rice vinegar
I 1/2 teaspoons Chinese oyster sauce
I 1/2 teaspoons mushroom soy sauce
I 1/2 tablespoons ketchup
3 pieces (each 1/2 inch long) fresh ginger

TANGERINE BEEF:

Cut beef across grain into paper-thin slices and trim to about I inch. Season to taste with salt and pepper. Dip into egg, then coat lightly with cornstarch. Heat I tablespoon oil in wok. Drop beef into oil to brown quickly. Remove and keep warm.

Add 2 tablespoons oil to wok. Add hot peppers, green onion and orange peel and sauté over high heat a few seconds. Pour Seasoning Sauce into wok all at once. Return beef mixture to wok. Mix well to heat thoroughly and quickly. Discard ginger from Seasoning Sauce. Serve immediately.

SEASONING SAUCE:

Combine sugar, soy sauce, vinegar, oyster sauce, mushroom soy sauce, ketchup and ginger in small bowl. Makes about 1/2 cup.

◆◆◆

4 servings. Each serving contains about: 330 calories; 1,012 mg sodium; 106 mg cholesterol; 21 grams fat; 15 grams carbohydrate; 20 grams protein; 0.79 gram fiber.

FLANK STEAK
Mandarette, Los Angeles

Readers say they are addicted to this easy, versatile dish of beef and flat noodles. Try substituting chicken, turkey, pork or even shellfish.

8 ounces beef flank steak
I tablespoon mirin or sake
I tablespoon soy sauce
1/2 teaspoon cornstarch
I egg white, beaten
1/4 teaspoon sugar
I teaspoon Chinese oyster sauce
I teaspoon hoisin sauce
2 tablespoons chicken broth
Pinch of black pepper
2 tablespoons vegetable oil
1/4 teaspoon pressed garlic
2 green onions, chopped
8 ounces flat rice noodles, cut into I-inch lengths

Cut beef into pieces about I 1/2 inches long and 1/2 inch thick. Place in bowl. Add mirin, I 1/2 teaspoons soy sauce, cornstarch and egg white. Mix well and set aside.

Combine sugar, remaining soy sauce, oyster sauce, hoisin sauce, chicken broth and pepper in another bowl. Mix well and set aside.

Heat I 1/2 tablespoons oil in wok over high heat. Add beef mixture and quickly sauté until lightly browned. Remove beef. Add remaining oil to wok and heat. Sauté garlic until golden brown. Add green onions, beef, rice noodles and reserved oyster sauce mixture and stir to blend. Cook until slightly thickened; do not overcook.

2 servings. Each serving contains about: 681 calories; 1,025 mg sodium; 43 mg cholesterol; 21 grams fat; 100 grams carbohydrate; 21 grams protein; 0.21 gram fiber.

❖ *Chef's Tip*: Flat rice noodles, which come in soft (fresh, not dry) white slabs, are available in most Chinese markets. A slab can be cut into any shape desired.

SKYLINE CHILI

Skyline Chili, Cincinnati, Ohio

In the Midwest, chili served over hot dogs and spaghetti is often named for the chili parlor that created it.

2 pounds ground beef
3 cups water
I can (15 ounces) tomato sauce
1/4 teaspoon garlic powder
2 bay leaves
I onion, chopped
I teaspoon cinnamon
I teaspoon Worcestershire sauce
I 1/2 teaspoons salt
2 teaspoons ground cumin
I 1/2 teaspoons red wine vinegar
I tablespoon chili powder
I 1/2 teaspoons ground allspice
1/2 teaspoon crushed red pepper

Mix ground beef and water in pot until well incorporated. Simmer until meat is cooked through, 20 to 25 minutes. Mix in tomato sauce, garlic powder, bay leaves, onion, cinnamon, Worcestershire sauce, salt, cumin, vinegar, chili powder, allspice and red pepper. Cook, uncovered, 3 hours, stirring occasionally. Remove bay leaves before serving.

◆◆◆

Each serving contains about: 233 calories; 442 mg sodium; 64 mg cholesterol; 18 grams fat; 2 grams carbohydrate; 15 grams protein; 0.30 gram fiber.

POOR MAN'S PEPPER STEAK
Dal Rae Restaurant, Pico Rivera

This version of steak au poivre uses ground beef patties instead of sirloin or other steak.

STEAK:
2 pounds ground beef
Coarsely ground black pepper
4 tablespoons butter
1/4 cup diced white onion
4 cups chopped green onions, mostly white parts
I cup chopped bacon
3 to 4 tablespoons finely chopped black peppercorns

BROWN SAUCE:
2 tablespoons concentrated beef demiglace
1/4 cup water
I cup beef broth

STEAK:
Shape ground beef into 4 oblong patties about I inch thick. Press layer of coarsely ground black pepper into both sides of patties.

Melt 2 tablespoons butter in skillet over medium-high heat. Add patties and diced onion and pan-fry, turning once, about 8 minutes for medium rare, 9 to 10 minutes for medium, or II to 12 minutes for well done. Remove from heat and set aside.

Melt remaining 2 tablespoons butter in another skillet over medium heat. Add green onions, bacon and chopped black pepper and sauté until bacon is crisp, about 10 minutes. Set aside.

Reheat patties in skillet. Top each patty with Brown Sauce and 3 tablespoons bacon-onion mixture. Serve at once.

BROWN SAUCE:
Stir demiglace paste into water until dissolved.

Heat broth in small saucepan. Stir in demiglace mixture and bring to boil. Reduce heat and simmer 5 minutes.

◆◆◆

4 servings. Each serving contains about: 652 calories; 547 mg sodium; 169 mg cholesterol; 54 grams fat; 7 grams carbohydrate; 33 grams protein; 0.48 gram fiber.

LAMB SHANKS

Musso & Frank Grill, Hollywood

Musso & Frank has been serving this dish for ages, and readers have been requesting it for almost as long.

4 lamb shanks
I clove garlic, minced
Salt, pepper
8 medium carrots, cut into I-inch pieces
8 small white onions
8 button mushrooms, caps only
8 small slices celery
I can (8 ounces) tomato sauce
I cup peas

Preheat oven to 350 degrees. Sprinkle lamb shanks with garlic and season to taste with salt and pepper. Bake 30 minutes, turning frequently to brown all sides. Add carrots, onions, mushrooms, celery and tomato sauce. Raise heat to 375 degrees and bake until meat is tender, about 45 minutes to I hour, adding peas after 30 minutes.

◆◆◆

4 servings. Each serving contains about: 266 calories; 498 mg sodium; 31 mg cholesterol; 12 grams fat; 29 grams carbohydrate; 13 grams protein; 6.96 grams fiber.

INDONESIAN RACK of LAMB

Trader Vic's, Beverly Hilton Hotel, Beverly Hills

Trader Vic's Indonesian Rack of Lamb is one of those recipes that readers follow from generation to generation. It's the consummate party entree and one of the restaurant's signature dishes. The peanut sauce is optional.

LAMB:
3/4 cup vegetable oil
1/3 cup finely chopped celery
1/3 cup finely chopped onion
I clove garlic, minced
1/2 cup rice vinegar
2 teaspoons steak sauce
3 tablespoons curry powder
2 dashes hot pepper sauce
3 tablespoons honey
I teaspoon dried oregano
2 bay leaves
1/2 cup prepared mustard
Juice and grated zest of I large lemon
I 6-chop rack of lamb or 6 lamb chops

LAMB:
   Heat oil in skillet and sauté celery, onion and garlic until translucent. Add vinegar, steak sauce, curry powder, hot pepper sauce, honey, oregano, bay leaves, mustard and lemon juice and zest. Bring to boil, reduce heat and simmer 2 minutes. Let cool, then chill.
   Add lamb rack or chops to mixture. Cover and marinate in refrigerator about 4 hours. Drain. Preheat oven to 400 degrees. Wrap bones with foil, leaving only meat exposed. Place lamb in shallow baking pan. Brush meat with marinade and roast about 20 minutes or longer, depending on thickness of meat and desired doneness; turn meat once and baste frequently with marinade. Place under broiler to brown top of meat, if necessary. Serve with Peanut Sauce, if desired.

PEANUT SAUCE:
1 cup peanut butter
1 cup canned coconut cream
Juice of 1/2 large lemon
1/4 cup soy sauce
1 tablespoon Worcestershire sauce
Dash of hot pepper sauce
1/4 teaspoon salt

Combine peanut butter, coconut cream, lemon juice, soy sauce, Worcestershire, hot pepper sauce and salt. Mix well and serve at room temperature. Makes about 2 cups.

◆◆◆

6 servings. Each serving, without peanut sauce, contains about: 249 calories; 319 mg sodium; 46 mg cholesterol; 15 grams fat; 15 grams carbohydrate; 15 grams protein; 2.41 grams fiber.

PORK CHOPS with TOMATO SAUCE

Il Gazebo, Glendale

The sautéed pork chops are butterflied with the bone intact and served over the tomato sauce for an impressive presentation.

3 tablespoons olive oil
3 tablespoons butter
4 rib pork chops, 6 ounces each
Salt, pepper
1/2 cup white wine
1/2 cup chicken broth
2 cloves garlic, minced
4 fresh sage leaves
10 to 12 black Italian olives, pitted and crushed
2 teaspoons capers
4 plum tomatoes, diced
1 cup pureed tomatoes or tomato sauce
1 teaspoon chopped fresh oregano leaves or 1/2 teaspoon dried

Heat olive oil and butter in large skillet over medium heat until butter melts. Add pork chops and cook until browned on both sides. Reduce heat, cover and cook over low heat 6 to 7 minutes or until pork chops are done. (If skillet is not large enough, cook chops in batches.) Season to taste with salt and pepper. Set aside.

Add wine and broth to skillet, scraping up brown bits from bottom of pan. Bring to vigorous boil and boil until reduced to glaze. Add garlic, sage, olives and capers.

Cover and simmer over low heat 6 to 7 minutes or until garlic is tender. Add diced tomatoes, pureed tomatoes and oregano and season to taste with salt and pepper. Bring to boil, reduce heat and simmer until thickened, about 15 minutes.

Butterfly cooked pork chops, leaving bone intact. Return chops to pan and heat through. Serve butterflied pork chops in center of plate with tomato sauce.

◆◆◆

4 servings. Each serving contains about: 353 calories; 861 mg sodium; 44 mg cholesterol; 32 grams fat; 6 grams carbohydrate; 8 grams protein; 1.57 grams fiber.

VEAL MARSALA

Mario's Cooking for Friends, Los Angeles

According to owner Mario Martinolli, the secret to successful veal Marsala is cooking the veal quickly and at a high temperature, which seals the thin outer layer of meat without overcooking the inside. The restaurant is no longer, but Mario generously shares recipes on his local radio talk show.

Olive oil
8 ounces mushrooms, cleaned and quartered
Salt, pepper
12 ounces veal scallops, cut across grain, pounded
All-purpose flour
1/2 cup Marsala
1/2 cup chicken broth
2 tablespoons chopped flat-leaf parsley
I tablespoon unsalted butter

Heat 2 tablespoons olive oil in skillet over medium heat. Add mushrooms, season to taste with salt and pepper and cook until liquid is absorbed and mushrooms are tender. Remove from skillet.

Barely cover bottom of skillet with olive oil. Heat until slightly smoking. Dredge veal in flour to dust lightly, then add to pan. Sear no more than 30 seconds on each side, seasoning to taste with salt and pepper. Remove from heat and set aside on heated platter.

Heat same skillet and add cooked mushrooms. When hot, add Marsala and boil until reduced by half. Add chicken broth and reduce by half. Add parsley, then stir in butter just until melted. Adjust seasonings to taste. Pour over veal and serve immediately.

4 servings. Each serving contains about: 362 calories; 234 mg sodium; 122 mg cholesterol; 19 grams fat; 9 grams carbohydrate; 34 grams protein; 0.5 gram fiber.

OSSO BUCO

Mi Piace, Pasadena

Mi Piace's recipe for authentic osso buco includes the traditional gremolata, the Italian word for the flavor-enhancing topping of lemon zest, parsley and garlic.

6 veal shanks
I cup all-purpose flour
3 tablespoons olive or vegetable oil
5 ounces mushrooms, quartered
2 carrots, diced
2 stalks celery, diced
I onion, diced
I cup diced peeled eggplant
$1/2$ fennel bulb, trimmed and diced (about I cup)
2 tablespoons chopped garlic
I cup red wine
$1/2$ cup tomato paste
6 cups reduced-sodium beef broth
2 bay leaves
Salt, pepper
2 tablespoons butter
3 tablespoons grated lemon zest
I tablespoon minced fresh parsley
$1/2$ teaspoon minced garlic

Dredge veal shanks in flour and shake off excess.·

Heat oil in Dutch oven over medium-high heat until it begins to smoke. Add shanks and sear until browned on all sides, 3 to 5 minutes per side. Remove and pat off excess oil.

Reduce heat to medium and add mushrooms, carrots, celery, onion, eggplant, fennel and garlic to Dutch oven. Sauté until softened and evenly browned, about 8 minutes. Add wine and cook over medium-high heat to deglaze pan, scraping brown bits from bottom of pan, I to 2 minutes.

Preheat oven to 325 degrees. Return shanks to pan. Whisk together tomato paste and beef broth and add to pan. Add bay leaves and salt and pepper to taste. Cover and bake until meat is tender and pulls away from bone, about I1/2 hours. Remove shanks from pan and keep warm.

Bring liquid remaining in pan to boil over medium-high heat and cook until reduced by half, about 10 minutes. Add butter and swirl until melted. Pour over shanks.

Combine lemon zest, parsley and garlic. Divide shanks among serving plates and sprinkle with lemon zest mixture.

◆◆◆

6 servings. Each serving contains about: 341 calories; 1,810 mg sodium; 56 mg cholesterol; 12 grams fat; 32 grams carbohydrate; 21 grams protein; 1.12 grams fiber.

VEGETABLES

◆◆◆

L et's face it: This chapter is filled with some of the most exotic, unusual, daring vegetable dishes anyone could dream up. On jaunts out of town, readers discover specialties like Mushroom Stroganoff and Vegetarian Moussaka. Ethnic restaurants do their part, too. Chinese Spicy Eggplant and Braised Long Beans, and Tofu Steak from a Japanese sushi restaurant, have become standard recipes in the "Culinary SOS" repertoire.

It's hard to resist trying them all. From party buffets to the Thanksgiving table, there's a festive occasion waiting for every single vegetable dish in this chapter.

Braised Long Beans ◆ Szechwan Chinese Restaurant

Green Corn Tamales ◆ El Cholo

Carrot Soufflé ◆ Chasen's

Creamed Spinach ◆ Saddle Peak Lodge

Spicy Eggplant ◆ Yang Chow

Eggplant Parmigiana ◆ De Mario's Cafe and Pizzeria

Mushroom Stroganoff ◆ Kilmorey Lodge Restaurant

Mexican Potatoes ◆ Acapulco Mexican Restaurants

Potatoes Romano ◆ The Original Enterprise Fish Co.

Breakfast Potatoes ◆ Cliff House

Candied Yams ◆ Aunt Kizzy's Back Porch

Black Bean Burgers ◆ Getty Museum Cafe

Vegetable Burger ◆ Columbia Bar & Grill

Lasagna di Verdura ◆ Il Mito

Pasta e Fagioli ◆ Spiga Trattoria

Tofu Steak ◆ Mako Sushi

Vegetable Curry ◆ Chan Dara

Vegetarian Moussaka ◆ Zeus & Co.

BRAISED LONG BEANS

Szechwan Chinese Restaurant, Lomita

The Chinese method of cooking long beans can be applied to most any familiar vegetable, such as green beans, asparagus, broccoli or cauliflower. Chinese vegetable preserve and dried shrimp are available at Asian markets.

I cup vegetable oil
1 1/2 pounds Chinese long beans, cut in half
1/4 cup chicken broth
I teaspoon cornstarch
I teaspoon Asian sesame oil
2 teaspoons minced dried shrimp
2 teaspoons minced Chinese vegetable preserve (optional)
4 cloves garlic, minced
I teaspoon minced fresh ginger
1 1/2 teaspoons sugar
I tablespoon soy sauce
I teaspoon white or rice vinegar
2 green onions, minced

Heat oil in large skillet to 375 degrees. Drop in beans in small batches and fry I minute. Remove with slotted spoon. Drain on paper towels. (Beans can be fried several hours ahead of time.)

Mix chicken broth with cornstarch and set aside.

Heat wok over high heat and add sesame oil. Add shrimp, vegetable preserve, garlic, ginger, sugar, soy sauce, vinegar, onions and cornstarch mixture and sauté I minute. Add fried long beans and cook until mixture has thickened slightly and beans are coated with sauce, 2 to 3 minutes. Serve immediately.

6 servings. Each serving contains about: 99 calories; 248 mg sodium; 8 mg cholesterol; 6 grams fat; II grams carbohydrate; 4 grams protein; I.3I grams fiber.

GREEN CORN TAMALES
El Cholo, Los Angeles

These are traditional holiday fare for many in Southern California. They are also wonderful for lunch or as a main dish with beans and rice.

12 ears yellow corn
3/4 cup cornmeal
1/4 cup shortening
1/4 cup (1/2 stick) butter
1/4 cup sugar
1/4 cup half and half or whipping cream
Salt
12 ounces Cheddar cheese, cut into 24 equal strips
I can (12 ounces) green chiles, cut into strips
Parchment paper

Cut off both ends of ears of corn. Remove husks and reserve for wrapping. Cut corn kernels off cobs. Grind kernels with cornmeal in food processor. Set aside.

Cream shortening with butter until creamy. Add sugar, half and half and salt to taste. Blend in corn mixture.

For each tamale, overlap 2 cornhusks lengthwise. Spread 1/4 cup corn mixture on husks to within I inch of edges. Place I cheese strip and I chile strip over filling. Top with 2 tablespoons corn mixture. Bring edges of cornhusks over filling to cover completely.

Place each tamale on 9-inch square of parchment paper. Fold in ends of cornhusks, then fold sides of parchment over tamale and fold up ends. Tie into neat package with string. Continue until all tamales are prepared.

Place tamales on steamer rack and steam I inch above simmering water about 40 minutes or until packets are firm and spongy. Serve hot.

24 tamales. Each tamale contains about: 149 calories; 292 mg sodium; 21 grams cholesterol; 8 grams fat; 15 grams carbohydrate; 5 grams protein; .4 gram fiber.

CARROT SOUFFLÉ

Chasen's, Beverly Hills

The now-closed Chasen's restaurant served this carrot soufflé as a side dish.

1 1/2 pounds carrots
Butter
Sugar
1/4 cup chopped onion
1/3 cup all-purpose flour
1/2 teaspoon salt
1/4 teaspoon nutmeg
1 cup milk
2 tablespoons packed light brown sugar
1/4 cup apple or orange juice
6 eggs, separated
3/4 teaspoon cream of tartar

Slice carrots 1 inch thick and steam until very tender, about 15 minutes. Puree in blender or food processor.

Butter bottom and sides of 13 x 9-inch baking dish. Sprinkle with sugar. In saucepan, cook onion in 1/3 cup butter over medium heat until tender but not brown, about 2 minutes. Blend in flour, salt and nutmeg and cook, stirring constantly, until mixture is smooth and bubbly. Stir in milk all at once. Add brown sugar and cook, stirring constantly, until mixture boils and thickens. Remove from heat. Blend in mashed carrots and apple juice.

Preheat oven to 350 degrees. Beat egg whites with cream of tartar in large mixing bowl at high speed until stiff but not dry.

Beat egg yolks slightly in small bowl. Blend small amount of hot carrot mixture into yolks. Stir yolk mixture into carrot mixture. Gently but thoroughly fold yolk mixture into whites. Pour into prepared baking dish and gently smooth surface.

Bake until puffy and delicately browned, 40 to 45 minutes. Serve immediately.

Each serving contains about: 406 calories; 671 mg sodium; 366 mg cholesterol; 25 grams fat; 33 grams carbohydrate; 14 grams protein; 1.57 grams fiber.

CREAMED SPINACH
Saddle Peak Lodge, Calabasas

Creamed spinach flavored with Pernod would make an enthusiastic spinach eater of anyone.

3 pounds fresh spinach, stemmed
I tablespoon butter
I tablespoon chopped shallot
3 cups heavy whipping cream
Salt, pepper
I tablespoon Pernod

Blanch spinach in large pot of boiling salted water about 3 minutes. Remove with slotted spoon and plunge into ice water to stop cooking and maintain green color. Drain.

Place spinach in cheesecloth and wring out excess water. Chop spinach coarsely or finely, as desired. Set aside.

Melt butter in large skillet and sauté shallot I minute. Add I 1/2 cups cream and bring to slow simmer. Add half of spinach, stirring slowly with whisk. Add remaining cream and spinach and simmer, stirring occasionally, until cream is reduced and thickened, about 15 minutes. Season to taste with salt and pepper. Stir in Pernod.

◆◆◆

8 servings. Each serving contains about: 362 calories; 209 mg sodium; 128 mg cholesterol; 35 grams fat; 8 grams carbohydrate; 6 grams protein; 1.40 grams fiber.

❖ *Chef's Tip*: Three 10-ounce packages frozen chopped spinach, thawed, can be substituted. Do not cook; place spinach in cheesecloth and wring out as much liquid as possible, then proceed with recipe.

SPICY EGGPLANT
Yang Chow, Los Angeles

Readers just can't get enough Chinese spicy eggplant in hot garlic sauce these days. Sometimes it's served as one of a procession of vegetable dishes on a banquet menu.

Vegetable oil
1 pound Japanese eggplant, peeled and cut into 3 x 1-inch pieces
1/4 teaspoon minced fresh ginger
1/4 teaspoon minced garlic
6 ounces ground pork or chicken
1/2 cup shredded bamboo shoots
2 tablespoons mirin or sweet white wine
1/3 cup chicken broth
2 tablespoons soy sauce
2 teaspoons sugar
1 teaspoon rice vinegar
Chile oil
1 1/2 teaspoons cornstarch
1 tablespoon water
1 teaspoon minced green onion
5 drops Asian sesame oil

Heat 1/2 cup vegetable oil in wok. Add eggplant and fry until golden, about 2 to 3 minutes. Remove from pan and drain on paper towels.

Combine 1 teaspoon vegetable oil, ginger and garlic in wok and heat. Add pork, bamboo shoots, wine, broth, soy sauce, sugar, vinegar and chile oil to taste. Bring to boil, stirring.

Add eggplant and toss to coat well. Bring to boil and cook 30 seconds longer. Mix cornstarch with water, stir into sauce mixture and cook 30 seconds. Remove from heat and add green onion and sesame oil. Serve immediately.

2 main course or 3 to 4 appetizer servings. Each main-course serving contains about: 399 calories; 1,183 mg sodium; 41 mg cholesterol; 28 grams fat; 24 grams carbohydrate; 15 grams protein; 2.54 grams fiber.

EGGPLANT PARMIGIANA
De Mario's Cafe and Pizzeria, Dana Point

De Mario's Cafe built a reputation on grandmother's Eggplant Parmigiana. It can be served as a first course or main dish.

Olive or vegetable oil
2 cloves garlic, sliced
I can (32 ounces) plum tomatoes, pureed
I teaspoon chopped fresh parsley
Pinch of hot pepper flakes
Salt, pepper
I cup all-purpose flour
I medium eggplant, peeled and cut into 1/4-inch-thick slices
3 eggs
2 tablespoons cold water
I package (8 ounces) mozzarella cheese, shredded

Heat 1/4 cup oil in saucepan. Add garlic and sauté until lightly browned. Add tomato puree, parsley, hot pepper flakes and salt and pepper to taste. Simmer over low heat I hour.

Place flour in large plastic food bag. Add eggplant slices one at a time and shake to coat with flour.

Beat eggs with cold water and salt and pepper to taste in shallow container. Dip floured eggplant slices in egg mixture.

Heat I cup oil in skillet. Add eggplant slices in batches and fry until golden brown on both sides. Remove from pan and drain on paper towels.

Preheat oven to 350 degrees. Cover bottom of 13 x 9-inch baking dish with 1/3 of tomato sauce. Place layer of fried eggplant slices over sauce and top with half of remaining sauce. Sprinkle with 1/3 of mozzarella. Repeat layers with remaining eggplant slices, sauce and cheese, ending with cheese. Bake 10 minutes. Cover pan with foil and bake 30 minutes longer.

◆◆◆

6 servings. Each serving contains about: 384 calories; 472 mg sodium; 136 mg cholesterol; 25 grams fat; 27 grams carbohydrate; 15 grams protein; 1.53 grams fiber.

MUSHROOM STROGANOFF

Kilmorey Lodge Restaurant, Alberta, Canada

A reader traveling through Waterton Lakes National Park in Alberta, Canada, discovered this sturdy side dish. It's also good as a main dish with wild rice and steamed vegetables.

2 tablespoons olive oil
1 1/2 pounds small white mushrooms, trimmed
1/4 cup chopped celery
1/4 cup chopped white onion
1/4 cup dry white wine
1 tablespoon chopped fresh basil
Salt, pepper
2 cups sour cream
1/4 cup whipping cream

Heat oil in large skillet. Add mushrooms, celery and onion and sauté just until browned. Add wine, basil and salt and pepper to taste. Cook, stirring, until sauce is reduced by 2/3.

Add sour cream and cook until reduced to consistency of cream sauce. Stir in whipping cream. Serve hot.

◆◆◆

4 servings. Each serving contains about: 415 calories; 155 mg sodium; 72 mg cholesterol; 37 grams fat; 15 grams carbohydrate; 8 grams protein; 1.38 grams fiber.

MEXICAN POTATOES

Acapulco Mexican Restaurants

From a popular Mexican restaurant chain comes this unusual and easy potato side dish.

6 tablespoons vegetable oil
5 baking potatoes, peeled and cut into 1/2-inch cubes
2 large green bell peppers, seeded and cut into 1/4-inch strips
2 onions, thinly sliced
1 large tomato, cut into 1/4-inch dice
1 teaspoon minced garlic
1 1/2 teaspoons salt
1/2 teaspoon pepper
2/3 cup (2 ounces) shredded Monterey Jack cheese
2/3 cup (2 ounces) shredded Cheddar cheese

Heat oil in large nonstick skillet over medium heat. Add potatoes and cook, stirring frequently, until barely tender, about 15 minutes. Add bell peppers, onions, tomato, garlic, salt and pepper and cook until onion is softened and potatoes are tender, about 10 minutes.

Preheat oven to 350 degrees. Spoon mixture into greased 13 x 9-inch baking dish or ovenproof casserole. Sprinkle cheeses over top. Bake 5 minutes or until cheeses melt. Serve immediately.

8 servings. Each serving contains about: 306 calories; 537 mg sodium; 14 mg cholesterol; 15 grams fat; 38 grams carbohydrate; 7 grams protein; 1.25 grams fiber.

POTATOES ROMANO

The Original Enterprise Fish Co., Santa Barbara

Here's a rather unusual potato casserole made with both diced and instant mashed potatoes. It makes a great side dish for a festive roast beef dinner.

2 1/2 pounds waxy potatoes, peeled and diced
I cup warm water
1/2 cup vegetable oil
2 1/4 cups nonfat dry milk
1/2 cup diced red bell pepper
I 1/2 teaspoons garlic powder
I 1/2 teaspoons white pepper
1/4 teaspoon seasoning salt
1/4 teaspoon salt
I cup instant mashed potatoes
Paprika
4 ounces Romano cheese, grated

Cook potatoes in boiling salted water just to cover until no longer crunchy, about 20 minutes. Set aside in cooking water.

In bowl of electric mixer combine I cup warm water, oil, dry milk, red pepper, garlic powder, white pepper, seasoning salt and salt. Add cooked potatoes with enough cooking liquid to mix thoroughly. Add instant mashed potatoes along with more cooking liquid as needed to form smooth consistency.

Preheat oven to 350 degrees. Transfer mixture to 3-quart casserole. Sprinkle with paprika to taste and top with Romano cheese. Bake until golden, I 5 to 20 minutes.

8 servings. Each serving contains about: 441 calories; 561 mg sodium; 25 mg cholesterol; 20 grams fat; 48 grams carbohydrate; 20 grams protein; 0.65 gram fiber.

BREAKFAST POTATOES

Cliff House, Playa del Rey

Though the Cliff House calls these cottage potatoes Breakfast Potatoes, they make a great accompaniment for barbecued roasts or grilled chicken or fish. They can also be conveniently reheated on the grill.

6 medium-size White Rose or other boiling potatoes
2 tablespoons butter
1 white onion, chopped
2 red bell peppers, seeded and diced
2 green bell peppers, seeded and diced
1/2 teaspoon garlic powder
1/2 teaspoon seasoned salt
1/2 teaspoon pepper

Preheat oven to 350 degrees. Bake potatoes 30 minutes. Refrigerate until cold (do not peel); slice potatoes when cold.

Melt butter in large skillet over medium heat and sauté onion and bell peppers until peppers are tender. Add garlic powder, seasoned salt and pepper. Add potatoes and sauté until potatoes are tender and flavors blend, about 10 minutes.

◆◆◆

8 servings. Each serving contains about: 107 calories; 120 mg sodium; 8 mg cholesterol; 3 grams fat; 19 grams carbohydrate; 2 grams protein; 1.70 grams fiber.

CANDIED YAMS
Aunt Kizzy's Back Porch, Marina del Rey

The ultimate candied yams served at Aunt Kizzy's Back Porch would make a major contribution to your holiday table. The restaurant advises picking sweet potatoes "with moist, dark orange flesh and skin ranging in color from almost purple to copper."

3 yams, about 2 1/2 pounds
I cup sugar
I 1/2 cups water
1/2 teaspoon nutmeg
Zest of 1/4 lemon, grated
1/4 cup (1/2 stick) butter
2 tablespoons lemon juice
I teaspoon vanilla extract

Scrub yams and place in large pot. Cover with boiling water and cook, covered, over medium heat until tender but still firm, 25 to 30 minutes. Drain and let cool.

Peel yams and cut into thick slices. Butter shallow 2-quart baking dish and arrange yam slices in single layer in dish.

Preheat oven to 425 degrees. Combine sugar, water, nutmeg and lemon zest in saucepan. Add butter and lemon juice. When butter melts, remove from heat and stir in vanilla. Pour syrup over yams in dish. Bake until bubbly, about 30 minutes.

◆◆◆

6 servings. Each serving contains about: 387 calories; 93 mg sodium; 21 mg cholesterol; 8 grams fat; 79 grams carbohydrate; 3 grams protein; 1.6 grams fiber.

BLACK BEAN BURGERS

Getty Museum Cafe, Los Angeles

A reader said her husband "really flipped" over the black bean burgers at the Getty Museum Cafe. So did we when we tested the recipe.

3 cans black beans (I pound each), rinsed and drained
1/4 cup chopped onion
1/2 cup chopped red bell pepper
I teaspoon cayenne pepper
I egg
Fine dry bread crumbs
2 tablespoons chopped cilantro
2 tablespoons olive oil
8 hamburger rolls
Salsa (optional)
Guacamole (optional)

Combine beans, onion, bell pepper, cayenne, egg, I cup bread crumbs and cilantro in food processor and blend, adding more bread crumbs as needed to make mixture dry enough to shape. Form into 8 patties. (Patties may be made a day ahead and refrigerated to help them set well.)

Heat I tablespoon olive oil in large skillet over medium heat. Add 4 patties and fry 2 minutes per side, turning once. Heat remaining oil and fry remaining 4 patties.

Place each patty in hamburger roll and serve with salsa and guacamole, if desired.

8 burgers. Each burger, without salsa or guacamole, contains about: 314 calories; 980 mg sodium; 50 mg cholesterol; 7 grams fat; 56 grams carbohydrate; 13 grams protein; 0.16 gram fiber.

VEGETABLE BURGER

Columbia Bar & Grill, Hollywood

This veggie burger, served on hamburger rolls with sliced tomato, pickle and lettuce, was a regular feature at the now closed Columbia Bar & Grill throughout the 1980s.

2 tablespoons butter
3 cups chopped mushrooms
I large onion, chopped
I cup rolled oats
I 1/2 cups shredded low-fat mozzarella cheese
I cup cooked brown rice
1/2 cup dry cottage cheese
3 eggs, beaten
I cup shredded Cheddar cheese
1/2 cup bulgur wheat, soaked in warm water to cover 20 minutes, squeezed dry
1/2 cup chopped walnuts
I tablespoon dried parsley
I tablespoon chopped fresh chives
Salt, pepper

Melt butter in large skillet over medium-high heat. Add mushrooms and onion and sauté until tender. Drain and cool. Transfer to bowl and mix in oats, mozzarella, rice, cottage cheese, eggs, Cheddar cheese, bulgur, walnuts, parsley and chives. Season to taste with salt and pepper. Cover and refrigerate overnight.

Divide mixture into 8 large or 12 smaller patties. Cook over medium coals, pan fry or broil until golden brown on both sides. Serve hot.

8 servings. Each serving contains about: 369 calories; 352 mg sodium; 104 mg cholesterol; 21 grams fat; 26 grams carbohydrates; 20 grams protein; 4.35 grams fiber; 9 grams saturated fat.

LASAGNA di VERDURA

Il Mito, Studio City

From a well-known Studio City restaurant, here's a meatless and pastaless lasagna using eggplant and peppers. Once the sauce and vegetables are prepped, it takes only a few minutes to assemble and bake the lasagna.

2 cups homemade tomato sauce
I large eggplant, cut into 1/4-inch-thick slices and grilled or broiled until tender
4 medium-size yellow bell peppers, roasted, peeled, seeded and sliced
I pound smoked mozzarella cheese, thinly sliced or shredded
4 medium-size red bell peppers, roasted, peeled, seeded and sliced
4 firm plum tomatoes, cut into 1/3-inch-thick slices
I cup freshly grated Parmesan cheese

Preheat oven to 375 degrees. Spread 1/2 cup tomato sauce in bottom of 12x7-inch baking dish. Layer with half of eggplant slices, half of yellow peppers, 1/3 of smoked mozzarella and half of red peppers. Top with another 1/3 of mozzarella slices and half of tomato slices.

Sprinkle with 1/3 of Parmesan. Pour I cup tomato sauce over. Repeat with remaining eggplant, yellow peppers, mozzarella, red peppers and tomatoes.

Sprinkle with another 1/3 of Parmesan. Spread with remaining 1/2 cup tomato sauce. Top with remaining Parmesan. Bake until hot and bubbling, 25 to 30 minutes.

◆◆◆

4 servings. Each serving contains about: 275 calories; 824 mg sodium; 42 mg cholesterol; 14 grams fat; 18 grams carbohydrate; 21 grams protein; 1.04 grams fiber.

PASTA e FAGIOLI

Spiga Trattoria, Costa Mesa

Pasta e fagioli, a classic pasta-and-bean soup-stew from Italy, is a rib-sticking meal to serve during Lent or any time.

I pound dried white kidney beans
I cup diced yellow squash
I cup diced zucchini
I cup diced carrots
I cup sliced leeks
I cup diced celery
2 cups diced peeled potatoes
Salt
Water or vegetable broth
8 ounces tube-shaped pasta

Soak beans overnight in about 4 quarts water.

Combine squash, zucchini, carrots, leeks, celery, potatoes and I teaspoon salt in large saucepan. Add water or vegetable broth to cover and bring to boil over high heat. Reduce heat and simmer until vegetables are tender, about 25 minutes. Remove from heat and let cool 20 minutes.

Puree vegetables and cooking liquid in batches in food processor. Set aside. Drain and rinse beans; place in large saucepan. Add 8 cups water and I teaspoon salt and bring to boil over high heat. Reduce heat and simmer, stirring frequently, until beans are tender, 30 to 40 minutes. Drain beans.

Combine beans and vegetable mixture and bring to boil over low heat. Add pasta and cook until pasta is al dente, 8 to I0 minutes. Season to taste with salt.

◆◆◆

6 servings. Each serving contains about: 369 calories; I44 mg sodium; 0 cholesterol; I gram fat; 72 grams carbohydrate; I9 grams protein; 4.59 grams fiber.

TOFU STEAK
Mako Sushi, Sherman Oaks

Japanese restaurants have been largely responsible for introducing tofu steak, a wonderful dish to keep in mind for nutritious meatless meals. Don't be intimidated by the use of two pans at once. You can stagger the cooking to avoid confusion, or practice cooking with two pans simultaneously, the way restaurant chefs often do.

1/2 cup olive oil
2 pounds sliced mushrooms
1/2 white onion, sliced
2 cartons (13 ounces each) extra-firm tofu, drained
1 1/2 cups cream sherry
3 tablespoons butter
1 teaspoon garlic powder mixed with 1 teaspoon water
3 tablespoons soy sauce

Heat 1/4 cup olive oil in 12-inch skillet over medium-high heat. Add mushrooms and onion and sauté until onion is tender, about 15 minutes.

Cut tofu into "steaks" by slicing each block into 3 lengthwise slabs. Heat 1/4 cup olive oil in second skillet over medium-high heat and sauté tofu steaks in batches until cooked on both sides, 4 to 5 minutes per side. Remove tofu and place steaks on top of cooked mushroom mixture in skillet.

Add sherry to pan that held tofu and heat. Tilt pan away from you and ignite sherry with long match, keeping face and loose clothing away from flames.

When flames die down, add butter and garlic powder mixture to skillet and heat until butter melts. Add soy sauce and simmer over medium heat until sauce thickens slightly, 3 to 4 minutes. Return tofu to pan and cook until lightly browned on both sides, 2 to 4 minutes per side.

Divide tofu among six serving plates and top with mushroom mixture and sauce. Serve hot.

6 servings. Each serving contains about: 496 calories; 589 mg sodium; 16 mg cholesterol; 35 grams fat; 17 grams carbohydrate; 24 grams protein; 1.48 grams fiber.

VEGETABLE CURRY

Chan Dara, Los Angeles

For those who enjoy experimenting with Thai cooking, making your own coconut milk from scratch might be worth the effort.

CURRY:
2 tablespoons vegetable oil
6 tablespoons Thai red chile paste or to taste
1 1/2 teaspoons curry powder
6 tablespoons nam pla (Thai fish sauce)
2 tablespoons sugar
6 cups Coconut Milk
2 carrots, sliced
1 potato, diced
6 leaves napa cabbage
1 onion, sliced
1 cup snow peas
2 cups broccoli spears
1/2 cup sliced mushrooms
6 ears baby corn
1/2 cup bamboo shoots

COCONUT MILK:
2 pounds grated coconut
12 cups hot water

CURRY:
Heat oil in skillet. Stir in chile paste, curry powder, fish sauce and sugar and cook over medium-high heat until flavors blend, about 2 minutes. Gradually add Coconut Milk, blending well. Bring to simmer. Add carrots and potato and simmer 10 minutes.

COCONUT MILK:
Blend grated coconut and water. Let cool to room temperature. Using cheesecloth, squeeze out cream to make about 6 cups coconut milk.

Add cabbage, onion, snow peas, broccoli, mushrooms, baby corn and bamboo shoots and simmer until broccoli is just tender, about 10 minutes. Serve immediately.

◆◆◆

8 servings. Each serving contains about: 536 calories; 643 mg sodium; 16 mg cholesterol; 46 grams fat; 30 grams carbohydrate; 7 grams protein; 4.32 grams fiber.

VEGETARIAN MOUSSAKA
Zeus & Co., Santa Barbara

You can substitute any vegetables you like in this moussaka. It makes a versatile dish for the vegetable lover.

MOUSSAKA:
2 large baking potatoes, peeled and cut into 1/4-inch-thick slices
1 large eggplant, cut into 1/4-inch-thick slices
3 zucchini, cut into 1/4-inch-thick slices
Olive oil
1 onion, chopped
1 cup cooked garbanzo beans
1 can (15 ounces) tomato sauce
Salt, pepper
Cinnamon
Nutmeg
1/4 cup bread crumbs, preferably from pita bread
1/3 cup grated Parmesan cheese

BECHAMEL SAUCE:
1/2 cup all-purpose flour
Cinnamon
Nutmeg
1/2 cup (1 stick) butter
1 quart milk
1/3 cup freshly grated Parmesan cheese

MOUSSAKA:
Brush potatoes, eggplant and zucchini with olive oil and grill until soft. Set aside.

Sauté onion in 2 tablespoons olive oil until soft. Stir in garbanzo beans, tomato sauce, salt, pepper, cinnamon and nutmeg to taste and heat through.

Preheat oven to 375 degrees. Grease 13 x 9-inch baking dish. Layer potato slices in prepared dish and sprinkle with bread crumbs. Spoon layer of tomato mixture over potatoes. Add layer of eggplant, then layer of tomato sauce. Follow with layer of zucchini slices, then remaining tomato sauce.

Spread top with Bechamel Sauce. Sprinkle with Parmesan. Bake until top is firm and lightly browned, about I hour. Serve hot.

BECHAMEL SAUCE:
Mix flour with cinnamon and nutmeg to taste. Melt butter in saucepan. Stir in flour mixture and cook 2 to 3 minutes. Add milk and cook, stirring, until thickened. Stir in cheese and keep warm until ready to use.

◆◆◆

6 to 8 servings. Each of 8 servings contains about: 432 calories; 775 mg sodium; 56 mg cholesterol; 25 grams fat; 38 grams carbohydrate; I7 grams protein; I.5I grams fiber.

PASTA, RICE & GRAINS

❖❖❖

A t one time, "Culinary SOS" readers considered pasta to be lowly stuff from delis, mom-and-pop restaurants and reader exchanges. It was good, but nothing special. Well, things changed for pasta—and even for rice and grains—as the health food movement, an explosion of modern French and Italian restaurants and an emerging California cuisine moved into the picture.

Today pasta holds a distinguished place on the menus of many top-rated restaurants. Hip California eateries offer such rarefied dishes as Penne with Lobster, and Fusilli with Sun-Dried Tomato Cream. Risotto, virtually unknown only a couple of decades ago, is now a hot number. It's not an easy dish to cook, but readers are learning how to stir the Italian Arborio rice in broth until it becomes creamy. Shrimp Risotto and Wild Mushroom Risotto are given here. You'll also enjoy the small, delectable rice croquettes, or Arancini di Riso, introduced as an appetizer or side dish by the Drago brothers, who operate several top Italian restaurants in L.A.

As for grains, the cornmeal mush called polenta is now in almost every savvy cook's vocabulary. The Polenta with Goat Cheese from the Getty Museum Cafe is an opulent version of a rustic staple.

Fettuccine Alfredo ◆ Talia's

Fusilli with Sun-Dried Tomato Cream ◆ Misto Caffe

Tequila Chicken Fettuccine ◆ Pizza Place

Gnocchi alla Nucca ◆ Osteria Romano Orsini

Penne alla Puttanesca ◆ I Cugini

Penne with Lobster ◆ Mezzaluna Ristorante

Arancini di Riso (Rice Croquettes) ◆ Il Pastaio

Coconut Rice ◆ Chan Darette

Shrimp Risotto ◆ Eclipse

Wild Mushroom Risotto ◆ Celestino

Polenta with Goat Cheese ◆ Getty Museum Cafe

Sweet Corn Cake ◆ El Torito Restaurants

Mexican Lasagna ◆ Lawry's California Center

Lentil Chili ◆ Nowhere Cafe

Lentil-Nut Loaf ◆ Mother's Market & Kitchen

FETTUCCINE ALFREDO

Talia's, Manhattan Beach

The secret of the velvety texture in this unusual Alfredo sauce is using cream cheese in lieu of the traditional Parmigiano-Reggiano. Wide fettuccine absorbs the thick sauce.

1/2 cup (1 stick) butter
12 ounces cream cheese
2 tablespoons sherry
Pinch of cayenne pepper
Pinch of white pepper
1/4 teaspoon garlic powder
2 cups half and half, plus more if needed
Salt
1 1/2 pounds wide fettuccine
1/4 cup minced Italian parsley

   Heat butter and cream cheese in saucepan over medium heat, stirring constantly, until cheese begins to melt. Add sherry, cayenne, white pepper and garlic powder. Vigorously whisk in 2 cups half and half until sauce is smooth and creamy. If too thick, add more half and half. Season with salt to taste.
   Cook fettuccine in boiling salted water 7 to 10 minutes. Drain. Stir parsley into sauce and toss with hot noodles. Serve immediately.

6 servings. Each serving contains about: 868 calories; 409 mg sodium; 133 mg cholesterol; 46 grams fat; 91 grams carbohydrate; 21 grams protein; 0.40 gram fiber.

FUSILLI with SUN-DRIED TOMATO CREAM

Misto Caffe, Torrance

The reader who requested this recipe found the dish "unforgettably rich and creamy." The rosy sauce is made with sun-dried tomatoes and cream.

1/4 cup olive oil
4 cloves garlic, roasted and chopped
1/2 large red onion, finely chopped
I pound boneless chicken breast, cooked, seasoned and diced
4 ounces bacon, cooked crisp and chopped
1/4 cup chopped fresh basil
2 ounces sun-dried tomatoes, reconstituted in water and chopped
3/4 cup dry white wine
I 3/4 cups heavy whipping cream
3 ounces Parmesan cheese, grated
Salt, pepper
2 pounds fusilli, cooked

Heat oil. Add garlic and onion and sauté until onion is translucent. Add chicken, bacon, basil and sun-dried tomatoes and sauté 10 minutes. Add wine and simmer until liquid is reduced by half. Add cream and Parmesan cheese and cook until sauce is reduced to creamy consistency. Season to taste with salt and pepper. Add to pasta and toss.

8 servings. Each serving contains about: 930 calories; 596 mg sodium; 140 mg cholesterol; 42 grams fat; 91 grams carbohydrate; 42 grams protein; 0.41 gram fiber.

TEQUILA CHICKEN FETTUCCINE

Pizza Place, San Gabriel

Try this with shrimp, lobster, scallops or leftover turkey as well as chicken.

2 tablespoons vegetable oil
2 pounds chicken thighs or other dark meat, boned and diced
2 red onions, cut into thin strips
2 red bell peppers, seeded and cut into thin strips
2 yellow bell peppers, seeded and cut into thin strips
2 green bell peppers, seeded and cut into thin strips
1 jalapeño, seeded and chopped
3 cloves garlic, minced
Tequila
1 1/2 cups chicken broth
1 1/2 cups whipping cream
Juice of 2 limes
Salt, pepper
1 bunch cilantro, chopped
1 1/2 pounds fettuccine
Cilantro sprigs

Heat oil in large skillet and brown chicken. Add onions, bell peppers, jalapeño and garlic and sauté 1 minute. Add 2 to 4 tablespoons tequila, or to taste, and chicken broth and cook over high heat until liquid is almost absorbed and pan is glazed.

Add cream and cook over medium-high heat until sauce thickens, about 7 to 8 minutes. Stir in lime juice, salt, pepper and chopped cilantro. Set aside.

Cook fettuccine in boiling salted water according to package directions; drain. To serve, top each plate of pasta with chicken-tequila sauce. Garnish with cilantro.

8 servings. Each serving contains about: 849 calories; 340 mg sodium; 158 mg cholesterol; 42 grams fat; 81 grams carbohydrate; 31 grams protein; 0.77 gram fiber.

GNOCCHI alla NUCCA

Osteria Romano Orsini, West Los Angeles

Using starchy baking potatoes makes for lighter gnocchi.

GNOCCHI:
10 medium baking potatoes
1 1/2 cups unbleached all-purpose flour
1 egg, lightly beaten
Freshly grated Parmesan cheese

BUTTER AND SAGE SAUCE:
1/2 cup (1 stick) butter
1 clove garlic, minced
1 tablespoon grated onion
6 sage leaves, cut into julienne

GNOCCHI:
Cook potatoes in boiling salted water until tender. Peel, then mash. Mound flour in large bowl or on work surface. Make well in center and place potatoes, egg and 2 tablespoons Parmesan in well. Gradually incorporate flour into ingredients in well, working mixture lightly until soft dough is formed.

Lightly roll dough into long cylinder. Cut into 4 portions. Lightly roll each portion into thin, pencil-like rod from center outward, using floured hands. Cut rods into 1/2-inch pieces and set aside.

Bring large pot of salted water to boil. Drop in gnocchi and simmer until dumplings rise to surface, about 6 to 8 minutes. Carefully remove gnocchi with slotted spoon and drain. Serve with Butter and Sage Sauce and sprinkle with Parmesan.

BUTTER AND SAGE SAUCE:
Melt butter in small skillet. Add garlic, onion and sage and sauté until sage changes color. Serve hot over gnocchi. Makes 1/2 cup.

6 servings. Each serving contains about: 455 calories; 218 mg sodium; 84 mg cholesterol; 18 grams fat; 66 grams carbohydrate; 9 grams protein; 3.92 grams fiber.

PENNE alla PUTTANESCA

I Cugini, Santa Monica

I Cugini uses ahi tuna and De Cecco pasta.

4 quarts water
I tablespoon coarse sea salt
I pound penne pasta
1/2 cup extra-virgin olive oil
I pound ahi tuna loin, cut into I 1/2-inch squares
2 tablespoons chopped garlic
2 teaspoons table salt
2 teaspoons freshly ground black pepper
2 teaspoons dried red pepper flakes
8 plum tomatoes, seeded and cut into 1/2-inch dice
1/4 cup capers
2 tablespoons halved pitted Kalamata olives
2 tablespoons halved pitted picholine olives
1/4 cup dry white wine
I can (8 ounces) tomato sauce
2 tablespoons finely chopped Italian parsley

Bring water to boil with sea salt. Add pasta and cook, stirring occasionally, until al dente, about 7 minutes. Drain and keep warm.

Heat 1/4 cup olive oil in nonstick skillet over high heat. Add tuna and sear about I minute per side. Remove tuna and keep warm.

Reduce heat to medium, add garlic to skillet and sauté until golden, about 30 seconds. Add table salt, pepper and red pepper flakes and cook 30 seconds. Add tomatoes, capers and olives and cook until liquid from tomatoes is reduced, about 3 minutes. Add wine and cook until absorbed, about 2 minutes. Add tomato sauce and cook 3 minutes. Add I tablespoon parsley and pasta. Carefully stir in reserved tuna. Toss with remaining 1/4 cup olive oil.

Serve in warm pasta bowls. Garnish each bowl with remaining parsley.

8 servings. Each serving contains about: 430 calories; 1,855 mg sodium; 17 mg cholesterol; 18 grams fat; 48 grams carbohydrate; 19 grams protein; 0.85 gram fiber.

PENNE with LOBSTER

Mezzaluna Ristorante, Corona del Mar

"My father was hardly able to keep his fork out of my plate. I would love the recipe in time for his birthday," wrote a good daughter. Mezzaluna promptly sent the recipe, and just in time for Dad's special day.

5 tablespoons olive oil
2 cloves garlic, I halved and I minced
1/2 medium-size red onion, chopped
I pound plum tomatoes, peeled and chopped
5 to 6 fresh basil leaves, chopped
I teaspoon sugar
Salt, pepper
I pound cooked lobster tail meat
I tablespoon chopped Italian parsley
8 ounces penne rigate or other tube-shaped pasta, cooked and drained

Heat 4 tablespoons olive oil and halved garlic clove in large saucepan over medium heat. Add onion and sauté until translucent. Remove and discard garlic. Add tomatoes, basil and sugar; season to taste with salt and pepper. Cook over low heat about I minute, stirring frequently. Remove from saucepan and puree in food processor or blender about 15 seconds.

Chop lobster meat into 3/4-inch cubes. Heat remaining I tablespoon olive oil in large skillet. Add minced garlic and sauté over high heat until translucent. Add lobster and continue cooking over high heat 2 minutes, stirring constantly. Add parsley and salt and pepper to taste. Add sauce from blender and cook I to 2 minutes longer. Toss penne with sauce and serve.

6 servings. Each serving contains about: 331 calories; 344 mg sodium; 54 mg cholesterol; 13 grams fat; 33 grams carbohydrate; 21 grams protein; 0.56 gram fiber.

ARANCINI di RISO (Rice Croquettes)
Il Pastaio, Beverly Hills

Use Italian Arborio rice; its high starch content helps hold the croquette in shape.

1/2 onion, finely chopped
1 tablespoon olive oil
2 cups Arborio rice
6 to 7 cups warm chicken broth
2 cups tomato sauce
1 tablespoon butter
1/4 cup freshly grated Parmesan cheese
Salt, pepper
3/4 cup finely diced provolone cheese
1/3 cup tomato-meat sauce
1/2 cup fresh or frozen peas
1/2 cup fine dry bread crumbs
Vegetable oil for deep frying

Heat olive oil in large skillet over medium heat. Add onion and sauté until softened, 2 to 3 minutes. Add rice and cook, stirring, until coated with oil. Add 1/2 cup chicken broth, bring to fast simmer and cook, stirring, until liquid is absorbed. Continue adding chicken broth 1/2 cup at a time, cooking and stirring until liquid is absorbed between additions. Cook until rice is al dente, about 20 minutes.

Add tomato sauce and continue cooking, stirring constantly, until rice is tender, 5 to 10 minutes. Mix in butter and Parmesan cheese. Rice should be dry, not runny; continue cooking to dry out mixture if necessary. Season to taste with salt and pepper. Let cool.

Place about 1/4 cup rice mixture in palm of hand and form into ball. Repeat with remaining rice mixture to make 24 croquettes. Make indentation in center of each ball with fingertip and fill pocket with provolone, meat sauce and peas. Form rice around filling in shape of bell or acorn. Repeat with remaining croquettes.

Roll croquettes in bread crumbs. Heat 2 inches oil in deep heavy skillet over medium heat. Drop croquettes into hot oil in batches without crowding pan. Cook until golden brown on all sides, about 5 minutes. Drain on paper towels and serve hot.

♦♦♦

24 croquettes. Each croquette contains about: 122 calories; 417 mg sodium; 4 mg cholesterol; 4 grams fat; 17 grams carbohydrate; 5 grams protein; 0.23 gram fiber.

COCONUT RICE

Chan Darette, Marina del Rey

Readers tell us that it's worth dining at the Chan Darette Thai Noodle Bar & Grill just for its coconut rice. It's usually served as an appetizer with sweet shredded beef jerky and spicy green papaya salad.

3 3/4 cups canned coconut milk
3 cups Basmati rice
1 cup milk, plus more if needed
1 tablespoon sugar
1 1/2 teaspoons salt
1 cup corn kernels, cooked black beans or pineapple chunks (optional)

Combine coconut milk, rice, milk, sugar and salt in large saucepan and simmer, stirring occasionally, until liquid is absorbed and rice is tender, about 30 minutes. Add up to 3/4 cup more milk if liquid evaporates before rice is cooked.

Stir in corn kernels, black beans or pineapple chunks, if desired for added flavor, before rice is completely cooked. Serve hot.

♦♦♦

8 servings. Each serving, without corn, beans or pineapple, contains about: 317 calories; 485 mg sodium; 2 mg cholesterol; 4 grams fat; 63 grams carbohydrate; 6 grams protein; 0.40 gram fiber.

SHRIMP RISOTTO
Eclipse, Beverly Hills

Eclipse is gone, but this risotto with its wonderfully rich, tasty seafood tomato sauce is memorable. Since the risotto takes time to prepare, you can have the tomato sauce simmering simultaneously, and both will be ready at about the same time.

RISOTTO:
12 ounces unpeeled shrimp
3 teaspoons olive oil
1 small clove garlic, minced
1/2 onion, chopped
1 cup Arborio rice
1/4 cup dry white wine
3 to 3 1/2 cups hot seafood broth
1 cup thinly sliced spinach
4 teaspoons butter
1 tablespoon chopped Italian parsley
1/4 cup freshly grated Parmesan cheese

SEAFOOD TOMATO SAUCE:
1 tablespoon olive oil
2 cups shrimp shells (from risotto)
1 1/3 cups chopped onion
1/2 cup chopped celery
1/3 cup chopped carrot
1 teaspoon chopped fresh thyme
Pinch of crushed dried red chile
Pinch of saffron
4 cloves garlic, minced
6 cups coarsely chopped tomato
4 cups water
1 cup dry white wine
1 tablespoon tomato paste

RISOTTO:

Peel shrimp, reserving shells for sauce. Cut shrimp into 1/4-inch pieces. Heat I tea-spoon olive oil in medium skillet. Add shrimp and stir-fry until shrimp turn pink, about 2 to 3 minutes. Remove and set aside.

Heat remaining oil in medium skillet. Add garlic and onion and sauté until tender. Add rice and sauté about I minute, tossing with wooden spoon.

Add wine and cook until wine evaporates, about 3 minutes. Add broth I cup at a time, stirring constantly between additions until broth completely evaporates, about 7 minutes for each cup. Cook until rice is tender but still chewy, about 25 minutes. If more liquid is needed, add hot water.

Line large bowl with spinach. Just before serving risotto, add shrimp pieces, but-ter, parsley and Parmesan cheese and mix well. Surround with Seafood Tomato Sauce.

SEAFOOD TOMATO SAUCE:

Heat olive oil in large saucepan over medium heat. Add reserved shrimp shells, onion, celery, carrot, thyme, chile, saffron and garlic and cook 3 to 5 minutes. Add tomato, water, wine and tomato paste and bring to boil. Reduce heat and simmer uncovered 35 minutes.

◆◆◆

6 servings. Each serving contains about: 381 calories; 617 mg sodium; 97 mg cholesterol; 11 grams fat; 43 grams carbohydrate; 21 grams protein; 1.87 grams fiber.

WILD MUSHROOM RISOTTO

Celestino, Beverly Hills

This recipe is a foodie's dream: lots of stirring, hip ingredients and flavor.

2 ounces dried porcini mushrooms
12 dried morel mushrooms
5 1/2 cups chicken broth
4 tablespoons butter
1 tablespoon chopped shallot
2 cloves garlic, minced
4 medium-size fresh shiitake mushrooms, sliced
1 cup dry white wine
Salt, pepper
1 3/4 cups Arborio rice
1 tablespoon mascarpone cheese
1/4 cup freshly grated Parmesan cheese
1 tablespoon chopped parsley

Soak dried mushrooms in just enough chicken broth to cover for 2 hours. Remove mushrooms from broth and squeeze dry. Chop mushrooms and set aside. Strain broth through paper coffee filter and reserve.

Melt 2 tablespoons butter in saucepan over medium heat. Add shallot, garlic, chopped mushrooms and shiitake and sauté 3 minutes. Add wine and cook until liquid is absorbed. Add reserved broth and cook until reduced by half, about 5 minutes. Add salt and pepper to taste. Set aside.

Bring remaining broth to simmer in saucepan; keep hot.

Melt 1 tablespoon butter in large skillet. Add rice and stir about 2 minutes to coat grains. Add 1/2 cup broth, stirring constantly with wooden spoon. Add another 1/2 cup broth and cook, stirring until rice becomes dry. Repeat adding broth in increments, cooking and stirring until rice is tender and all broth is used, about 25 minutes. Stir in mushroom mixture, mascarpone, 1 tablespoon butter and Parmesan. Add more salt and pepper if needed. Remove from heat and mix well. Sprinkle with parsley before serving.

6 servings. Each serving contains about: 436 calories; 885 mg sodium; 28 mg cholesterol; 12 grams fat; 64 grams carbohydrate; 12 grams protein; 4 grams fiber.

POLENTA with GOAT CHEESE

Getty Museum Cafe, Los Angeles

Served with roasted peppers or other vegetables, polenta topped with goat cheese is sturdy enough for a meatless main dish.

4 cups milk
I cup cornmeal
I tablespoon minced garlic
1/4 cup soft goat cheese
2 tablespoons chopped mixed fresh parsley, basil and chives
Salt, pepper

Bring milk to boil in saucepan over medium heat. Let simmer I minute, then whisk in cornmeal. Add garlic. When mixture begins to thicken, stir with wooden spoon until thick, about 5 minutes.

Add goat cheese, herbs and salt and pepper to taste.

◆◆◆

8 servings. Each serving contains about: 137 calories; 115 mg sodium; 11 mg cholesterol; 4 grams fat; 20 grams carbohydrate; 6 grams protein; 0.14 gram fiber.

SWEET CORN CAKE

El Torito Restaurants

Besides regular cornmeal, you'll need instant masa, the Mexican-style cornmeal from which tortillas and tamales are made. It is available at Mexican grocery stores and most supermarkets.

1/4 cup (1/2 stick) unsalted butter
2 tablespoons shortening
1/2 cup instant masa
3 tablespoons cold water
I package (10 ounces) frozen corn kernels
  or kernels from 2 large fresh ears of corn
3 tablespoons cornmeal
1/4 cup sugar
2 tablespoons whipping cream
1/4 teaspoon baking powder
1/4 teaspoon salt

Cream butter and shortening in mixing bowl until fluffy. Gradually mix in instant masa, then water.

Coarsely chop corn kernels in blender. Stir into masa mixture.

Mix cornmeal, sugar, cream, baking powder and salt in large bowl. Add masa mixture and blend well.

Preheat oven to 350 degrees. Grease 8-inch square pan. Pour masa mixture into prepared pan. Cover with foil and bake until firm, 40 to 50 minutes. Let stand at room temperature 15 minutes before cutting into squares, or use ice cream scoop to serve.

10 servings. Each serving contains about: 147 calories; 76 mg sodium; 16 mg cholesterol; 9 grams fat; 17 grams carbohydrate; 2 grams protein; 0.21 gram fiber.

MEXICAN LASAGNA

Lawry's California Center, Los Angeles

When a reader sent us this old recipe from Lawry's, we asked the restaurant to update it for us. This is their revamped version. It still makes a great family dish or party casserole.

1 1/2 pounds lean ground beef
1 envelope (1 ounce) taco seasoning mix
1/2 to 1 teaspoon seasoned salt
1 cup diced fresh or canned tomatoes
2 cans (8 ounces each) tomato sauce
1 can (4 ounces) diced green chiles
1 cup ricotta cheese
2 eggs, beaten
10 corn tortillas
2 1/2 cups (10 ounces) shredded Monterey Jack cheese

Cook ground beef in large skillet over medium heat until browned and cooked through, about 8 minutes. Drain off fat. Add taco seasoning mix, seasoned salt, tomatoes, tomato sauce and chiles. Mix well and bring to boil. Reduce heat and simmer, uncovered, 10 minutes.

Combine ricotta and eggs in small bowl.

Preheat oven to 350 degrees. Spread half of meat mixture in 13x9-inch baking dish. Arrange 5 tortillas over meat. Spread half of ricotta mixture over tortillas. Sprinkle with half of Jack cheese. Repeat layers.

Bake uncovered until cheese is melted and lightly browned, 20 to 30 minutes. Let stand 10 minutes before cutting into squares for serving.

8 servings. Each serving contain about: 494 calories; 945 mg sodium; 148 mg cholesterol; 31 grams fat; 25 grams carbohydrate; 29 grams protein; 1.99 grams fiber.

LENTIL CHILI
Nowhere Cafe, Hollywood

This vegetarian chili is ideal for a meatless menu. Serve it with warm tortillas and a veggie-packed salad. Vegetable stock can be made with stock base available in granule, paste or bouillon form at most markets.

I pound lentils
2 quarts vegetable broth or water, plus more if needed
2 cups diced onions
I cup crushed tomatoes
1/4 cup tomato paste
2 tablespoons chopped garlic
2 tablespoons balsamic vinegar
2 tablespoons lime juice
I tablespoon ground cumin
I tablespoon salt
2 tablespoons chili powder
I teaspoon cayenne pepper
Cilantro sprigs
Red onion slices

Combine lentils, broth, onions, tomatoes, tomato paste, garlic, vinegar, lime juice, cumin, salt, chili powder and cayenne in large saucepan and bring to boil over high heat.

Reduce heat, cover and simmer over medium-low heat until lentils are tender, about 30 to 35 minutes, adding more water or broth if needed for proper chili consistency.

Garnish each serving with sprig of cilantro and slice of red onion.

6 servings. Each serving contains about: 147 calories; 1,477 mg sodium; 0 cholesterol; I gram fat; 28 grams carbohydrate; 9 grams protein; 9.05 grams fiber.

LENTIL-NUT LOAF
Mother's Market & Kitchen, Costa Mesa

This loaf is a great alternative to turkey if you are looking for a vegetarian Thanksgiving.

1 1/4 pounds green lentils
1/2 cup sliced mushrooms
1/2 cup chopped onion
1/2 cup chopped mixed red and green bell pepper
1/2 cup fresh bread crumbs
1/2 teaspoon chopped fresh basil
1/2 teaspoon chopped fresh oregano
1/2 teaspoon chopped fresh thyme
1/2 teaspoon chili powder
Pepper
1 tablespoon tamari soy sauce
1 teaspoon salt
3/4 cup shredded fat-free mozzarella cheese
1/2 cup chopped walnuts
1/4 cup water
2 egg whites, beaten to soft peaks
Vegetable oil

Combine lentils, mushrooms, onion and bell pepper with water to cover in 4-quart saucepan and bring to boil over medium-high heat. Reduce heat and simmer until tender, about 1 hour. Drain lentil mixture and let cool 10 minutes.

Preheat oven to 350 degrees. Lightly grease 9-inch square pan. Mix lentil mixture with bread crumbs, basil, oregano, thyme, chili powder, pepper to taste, tamari, salt, mozzarella, walnuts and water. Gently stir in egg whites. Pour into pan, spreading evenly; mixture will fill pan.

Bake until lightly browned, about 30 minutes. Cool 15 minutes before cutting and serving.

12 servings. Each serving contains about: 226 calories; 343 mg sodium; 4 mg cholesterol; 5 grams fat; 30 grams carbohydrate; 17 grams protein; 2.82 grams fiber.

DESSERTS

◆◆◆

As you can see by the huge list of recipes in this chapter, our readers are no different than other folks who talk a good game about health and diet but can't keep away from desserts. So, let us give you the big picture—cakes, cheesecakes, cookies, fruit, pies, puddings, creams, soufflés.

Cake and cookie recipes take the popularity prize, and some of the most sought after are here. Have a look at the Ranger Cookies (also known as Flying Saucers, which are no longer available at Los Angeles public school cafeterias but remain the favorite of countless former students going back decades.

Among the cakes, readers adore the Daily Grill's Strawberry Shortcake, the Blum's Bakery Coffee Crunch Cake and Acapulco's Chocolate Chip Cheesecake.

An informal poll shows that more men than women request pudding recipes, for reasons we can only guess. How comforting puddings are. We've included a handful of the most popular ones in this chapter.

Our pie recipes "are to die for," as readers often tell us. Lawry's Coconut Banana Cream Pie, and a truck stop pie made with candy bars are top favorites.

Just a word to the wise. Desserts, especially baked desserts, depend on the perfect balance of ingredients for success, so we advise that you follow the recipes exactly. (You can substitute fruit juices for liquors or liqueurs, using the exact amounts of liquid called for.) Measure everything and be careful about baking times. Some ovens, if not calibrated, may bake more quickly or slowly than the recipe specifies. Let your nose and eye be your guide.

Almond Torte ✦ Hollywood Hills Coffee Shop/Cafe

Coffee Crunch Cake ✦ Blum's Bakery

Italian Rum Cake (Zuppa Inglese) ✦ Fratello's

Warm Chocolate Pudding Cake ✦ Shutters on the Beach

Malt Cake ✦ T.G.I. Friday's Restaurants

Pineapple-Coconut Cake ✦ Aunt Tizzy's Back Porch

Strawberry Shortcake ✦ Daily Grill

Banana Cake ✦ Montecito Cafe

Chocolate Chip Cheesecake ✦ Acapulco Mexican Restaurants

Date-Nut Cheesecake ✦ The Source

Espresso-Macadamia Nut Cookies ✦ Rock Restaurant

Haystacks ✦ Griswold's

Ranger Cookies (Flying Saucers) ✦ Los Angeles Unified School District

Krispy Rice Squares ✦ Getty Museum Cafe

Breakfast Cookies ✦ Julienne

Cafe Brownies ✦ Spotlight Cafe

Bananas and Strawberries Flambé ✦ Bacchanal Room

Tarte Tatin ✦ Joe's Restaurant

Butterscotch Dream Pie ✦ PJ's Restaurant

Truck Stop Reece Pie ✦ P&H Truck Stop

Tiramisù ✦ Boccaccio

Key Lime Pie ✦ Cafe del Sol

Coconut Banana Cream Pie ✦ Lawry's

Custard and Croissant Pudding ✦ Patina

Ginger Crème Brûlée ✦ Chaya Venice

Crema Catalana ✦ La Paella

Chocolate Soufflé ✦ Moustache Cafe

Capirotada ✦ Sonora Cafe

Crema di Vaniglia ✦ Il Moro

Deep Chocolate Pudding ✦ Vince & Eddie's

Chocolate Tart ✦ Rockenwagner

ALMOND TORTE

Hollywood Hills Coffee Shop/Cafe, Hollywood

Hollywood Hills Coffee Shop/Cafe sent us this surprisingly easy torte recipe. Almond paste is available in gourmet food stores and many supermarkets.

1/2 cup (1 stick) butter, softened
1 cup sugar
1 tube (7 ounces) almond paste, cut into small pieces (about 1 cup)
3 eggs
1/4 teaspoon amaretto
1/2 teaspoon Triple Sec or other orange liqueur
1 teaspoon baking powder
1 cup all-purpose flour
Powdered sugar

Preheat oven to 350 degrees. Grease and flour 8-inch round pan. Cream butter and sugar with electric mixer until fluffy, 1 to 2 minutes. Gradually blend in almond paste. Add eggs one at a time, beating well after each addition. Beat in amaretto and Triple Sec. Fold in baking powder and flour.

Pour batter into prepared pan and bake until torte is lightly browned, 35 to 45 minutes. Let cool slightly in pan, then invert onto cake rack. When completely cool, dust with powdered sugar.

◆◆◆

6 servings. Each serving contains about: 464 calories; 260 mg sodium; 148 mg cholesterol; 23 grams fat; 59 grams carbohydrate; 7 grams protein; 0.27 gram fiber.

COFFEE CRUNCH CAKE

Blum's Bakery, San Francisco

This has been a Times reader favorite for more than 35 years, almost as long as the column has been around. The praline brittle makes the cake, but if you don't have the time for this step, you can substitute store-bought brittle for almost the same effect. By the way, the bakery still features this cake.

1 1/2 cups sugar
1/4 cup strong brewed coffee
1/4 cup light corn syrup
1 tablespoon baking soda
1 store-bought angel-food cake (16 ounces)
2 cups whipping cream, whipped

   Combine sugar, coffee and corn syrup in medium saucepan at least 5 inches deep. Bring mixture to boil and cook until it reaches 310 degrees on candy thermometer or reaches hard-crack stage (when a small amount dropped into cold water breaks with a brittle snap).
   Press baking soda through sieve to remove lumps. Remove syrup from heat. Immediately add soda and stir vigorously just until mixture thickens and pulls away from sides of pan. (Mixture foams rapidly when soda is added. Do not destroy foam by beating excessively.)
   Immediately pour foamy mass, being careful to avoid spatters, into ungreased 9-inch square metal pan; do not spread or stir. Let stand without moving until cool, about 1 hour.
   When ready to garnish cake, remove brittle from pan and crush coarsely between sheets of wax paper with rolling pin.
   Frost cake with whipped cream. Cover generously and thoroughly with brittle pieces. Refrigerate until serving time.

12 servings. Each serving contains about: 351 calories; 79 mg sodium; 55 mg cholesterol; 15 grams fat; 53 grams carbohydrate; 3 grams protein; 0 fiber.

ITALIAN RUM CAKE (Zuppa Inglese)

Fratello's, West Los Angeles

Zuppa Inglese, which means "English soup" in Italian, probably goes back to the 19th century, when Britons touring Italy demanded trifle for dessert. You'll be surprised at how easy this dessert is to make the Fratello's way.

1 quart half and half
2 packages (3 1/2 ounces each) instant lemon pudding mix
1/2 cup finely chopped mixed candied fruit (optional)
1 frozen pound cake (10 3/4 ounces), thinly sliced
2 to 4 tablespoons rum, Marsala or vermouth (optional)
2 egg whites

Combine half and half with dry pudding mix and refrigerate until thickened. Fold in candied fruit if desired.

Preheat oven to 350 degrees. Cover bottom of 12-inch round, flat-bottomed oven-proof bowl or baking pan with half of cake slices. Spread pudding mixture over cake slices, covering completely. Layer remaining cake slices over top. Drizzle cake with rum if desired.

Beat egg whites until stiff. Spread over cake slices, covering completely. Bake until egg whites turn golden brown, about 12 minutes.

◆◆◆

6 servings. Each serving, without candied fruit, contains about: 610 calories; 476 mg sodium; 145 mg cholesterol; 35 grams fat; 64 grams carbohydrate; 10 grams protein; 1.00 gram fiber.

WARM CHOCOLATE PUDDING CAKE

Shutters on the Beach, Santa Monica

This made every chocoholic in the Times test kitchen gleeful after one taste. It's exceptional served with vanilla ice cream and caramel sauce.

15 ounces bittersweet chocolate
3/4 cup (1 1/2 sticks) butter
8 eggs, separated
2/3 cup sugar
4 ounces bittersweet or semisweet chocolate chunks or chips

Melt 15 ounces chocolate and butter in double boiler over simmering water until mixture is smooth. Do not let chocolate temperature rise above 100 degrees on candy thermometer. Let cool to 80 degrees.

Beat egg yolks with mixer until thick. Gradually beat in 1/3 cup sugar. Fold egg mixture into cooled chocolate.

Preheat oven to 350 degrees. Grease and flour 18 muffin cups. In separate bowl, beat egg whites until foamy. Add remaining 1/3 cup sugar, whipping until stiff peaks form. Fold egg white mixture into chocolate mixture. Add chocolate chunks. Divide batter among prepared muffin cups and bake until cake puffs up like soufflé, 25 to 30 minutes. While still warm, use rubber spatula to push sides of cakes toward center. Let cool 2 hours, then remove from pans. Serve at room temperature or rewarmed 20 seconds in microwave.

◆◆◆

18 pudding cakes. Each cake contains about: 241 calories; 69 mg sodium; 105 mg cholesterol; 19 grams fat; 20 grams carbohydrate; 5 grams protein; 0.58 gram fiber.

MALT CAKE
T.G.I. Friday's Restaurants

This classic malt cake has a cream cheese frosting flavored with malt powder. Malt powder and pasteurized egg yolks are available at most supermarkets.

MALT FROSTING:
1 package (12 ounces) semisweet chocolate chips
2 cups whipping cream
1 1/4 cups malt powder
1/3 cup sugar
4 ounces cream cheese, softened
1 teaspoon vanilla extract
2 tablespoons pasteurized egg yolks

CAKE:
1 cup plus 3 tablespoons vegetable oil
1/2 cup plus 2 tablespoons milk
1/2 cup plus 2 tablespoons plain yogurt
1/2 cup pasteurized egg yolks
1 tablespoon vanilla extract
3 cups sugar
3 cups all-purpose flour
3/4 cup plus 1 tablespoon unsweetened cocoa powder
1 1/2 tablespoons baking soda
1/2 teaspoon salt
1 1/4 cups boiling water

MALT FROSTING:
Melt chocolate chips over low heat, stirring constantly. Let cool.

Beat cream and malt powder with electric mixer at high speed until stiff, about 2 minutes. Refrigerate until cool, about 30 minutes.

Beat sugar, cream cheese and vanilla in separate bowl until creamy, about 2 minutes. Add egg yolks and beat 2 minutes more, scraping bowl often. Add chocolate and beat 1 more minute.

Add half of malt mixture and beat until uniform in color. Fold in remaining malt mixture with rubber spatula until frosting is uniform in color. Refrigerate at least 2 hours before icing cake.

CAKE:

Beat oil, milk, yogurt, egg yolks and vanilla with electric mixer until well blended, about 2 minutes.

Sift sugar, flour, cocoa powder, baking soda and salt in separate bowl.

Preheat oven to 300 degrees. Line bottoms of three 9-inch round pans with parchment or wax paper; butter and flour paper. Slowly add 1/3 of dry ingredients to milk mixture and mix until well blended. Beat in 1/3 of boiling water. Add another 1/3 of dry ingredients and mix well, then beat in another 1/3 of water. Beat in remaining dry ingredients, then add remaining water and beat well, scraping bowl often.

Divide batter equally among prepared pans. Bake until toothpick inserted in center comes out clean, 45 to 55 minutes; do not open oven during baking.

Cool layers in pans on racks 15 minutes. Turn layers out onto racks and cool completely. Fill and frost layers with Malt Frosting to make three-layer cake.

◆◆◆

10 servings. Each serving contains about: 1,064 calories; 87 mg sodium; 196 mg cholesterol; 63 grams fat; 128 grams carbohydrate; 10 grams protein; 0.83 gram fiber.

PINEAPPLE-COCONUT CAKE

Aunt Kizzy's Back Porch, Marina del Rey

When Aunt Kizzy's owner, Adolph Dulan, a social worker, married his colleague, Mary, there were some embellishments on the spectacular coconut cake served at the restaurant, but not many. "It's still basically the same cake as the one that came from my mother's log cabin and the one I ate for 56 years," says Dulan.

CAKE:

3 3/4 cups cake flour
5 1/4 teaspoons baking powder
1 1/2 teaspoons salt
1 cup (2 sticks) butter, at room temperature
2 1/2 cups sugar
4 eggs
1 3/4 cups milk
1 1/2 teaspoons vanilla extract
4 ounces flaked coconut
1 pineapple, peeled (optional)

FILLING:

1/2 cup (1 stick) butter
1 cup sugar
1 tablespoon cornstarch
2 cups drained crushed pineapple, juice reserved

TOPPING:

1 1/2 cups (3 sticks) butter, at room temperature
1 1/2 cups sugar
Reserved crushed pineapple juice as needed

CAKE:

Preheat oven to 350 degrees. Lightly butter bottoms and sides of three 10-inch round cake pans. Dust with flour.

Sift together flour, baking powder and salt three times. Cream butter and sugar with electric mixer. Beat in eggs one at time, blending well after each addition. Slowly blend in dry ingredients alternately with milk and vanilla and blend well. Divide batter equally among prepared pans.

Bake until wooden pick inserted in center comes out clean, about 30 to 40 minutes. Cool cakes on racks 5 minutes. Invert cakes onto racks and cool another 5 minutes.

Place first cake layer on 12-inch platter. Spread with half of Filling and sprinkle with 1 ounce flaked coconut. Add second cake layer, spread with remaining Filling and sprinkle with 1 ounce coconut. Add third layer and let stand 10 minutes. Cover top and sides with Topping. Sprinkle with remaining 2 ounces coconut.

Core and quarter pineapple. Cut each quarter into three triangles and place around base of cake.

FILLING:

Melt butter in saucepan over medium heat. Slowly add sugar and cornstarch, stirring constantly. Gradually add crushed pineapple and heat, stirring, until mixture thickens. Remove from heat. Makes about 2 1/2 cups.

TOPPING:

Cream butter and sugar until light and fluffy. If too thick, thin with pineapple juice reserved from Filling. Makes about 3 cups.

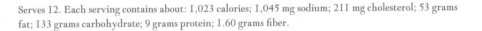

Serves 12. Each serving contains about: 1,023 calories; 1,045 mg sodium; 211 mg cholesterol; 53 grams fat; 133 grams carbohydrate; 9 grams protein; 1.60 grams fiber.

STRAWBERRY SHORTCAKE

Daily Grill, Los Angeles

This easy-to-make shortcake has been called the best in Los Angeles.

STRAWBERRY SAUCE:
I pound whole strawberries, hulled
1 1/2 cups water
1/2 cup sugar
Juice of I orange

SHORTCAKE:
1 1/2 cups biscuit mix
1/2 cup whipping cream
2 tablespoons sugar
3 baskets (1/2 pint each) strawberries, rinsed and sliced
   (reserve 4 whole berries for garnish)
I cup whipping cream, whipped

STRAWBERRY SAUCE:
   Combine strawberries, water, sugar and orange juice in saucepan and bring to boil, stirring occasionally. Reduce heat to low and cook 25 minutes. Cool, then chill. Puree in blender. Makes about 2 cups.

SHORTCAKE:
   Preheat oven to 375 degrees. Combine biscuit mix, 1/2 cup whipping cream and sugar in bowl and mix just until combined. Roll out to 1/2-inch thickness. Cut into four 3-inch rounds with cookie cutter. Arrange rounds on ungreased baking sheet. Bake until light brown, about 12 to 15 minutes. Let cool.

   For each serving, split one cake in half and place half on plate. Pour about 1/4 cup Strawberry Sauce over each shortcake. Place dollop of whipped cream and about 5 sliced strawberries on top of each cake. Top with small dollop of whipped cream.

   Top each shortcake with another half of shortcake and pour 1/4 cup Strawberry Sauce on top, then dollop with whipped cream and top with 5 more sliced strawberries. Garnish top with whole berry.

◆◆◆

4 servings. Each serving contains about: 691 calories; 562 mg sodium; 123 mg cholesterol; 40 grams fat; 80 grams carbohydrate; 6 grams protein; 1.26 grams fiber.

BANANA CAKE

Montecito Cafe, Santa Barbara

What a nice, moist banana cake for entertaining.

3 very ripe bananas, pureed (about I cup)
1/2 cup buttermilk
I teaspoon vanilla extract
3/4 cup (I 1/2 sticks) butter, at room temperature
I 1/2 cups sugar
2 eggs
2 cups sifted cake flour
I teaspoon baking soda
I teaspoon baking powder
1/2 teaspoon salt
Vanilla or chocolate buttercream frosting, as desired
Chopped toasted almonds (optional)

Beat banana puree, buttermilk and vanilla until well mixed. Set aside.

Cream butter, sugar and eggs until fluffy and pale in color. Set aside.

Preheat oven to 350 degrees. Line bottom of 9-inch springform pan with parchment paper; butter and flour parchment. Sift together flour, baking soda, baking powder and salt. Add dry ingredients to puree in three additions alternately with egg mixture, beating each time until well blended.

Pour batter into prepared pan. Bake until wooden pick inserted in center comes out clean, 50 to 55 minutes. Cool thoroughly in pan. When cool, invert cake onto plate and remove springform. Peel off parchment paper.

Split cake into 3 layers. Frost as desired and sprinkle top of cake with chopped almonds, if desired.

8 servings. Each serving, without frosting, contains about: 460 calories; 409 mg sodium; 100 mg cholesterol; 19 grams fat; 70 grams carbohydrate; 5 grams protein; 0.27 gram fiber.

CHOCOLATE CHIP CHEESECAKE

Acapulco Mexican Restaurants

Here's a holiday-time recipe from the Acapulco chain. It must be started several days ahead.

GRAHAM CRACKER CRUST:
10 tablespoons (1 ¼ sticks) butter or margarine, melted
2 cups graham cracker crumbs
3 tablespoons sugar

SOUR CREAM TOPPING:
½ cup sour cream
½ cup imitation sour cream
½ cup sugar
1 cup chocolate syrup

FILLING:
4 packages (8 ounces each) cream cheese, softened
1 cup sugar
2 eggs
¼ teaspoon lime juice
¼ teaspoon vanilla extract
8 ounces semisweet chocolate chips

GRAHAM CRACKER CRUST:
Preheat oven to 350 degrees. Blend butter, graham cracker crumbs and sugar. Press mixture against bottom and sides of 9-inch springform pan to within 1 inch of top edge. Bake 10 minutes. Let cool.

SOUR CREAM TOPPING:
Blend sour cream, imitation sour cream and sugar 5 minutes at medium speed of electric mixer. Add chocolate syrup and mix 3 minutes. Refrigerate until ready to use.

FILLING:

Preheat oven to 375 degrees. Blend cream cheese and sugar 5 minutes at medium speed of electric mixer. Beat in eggs, lime juice and vanilla and mix 5 minutes longer. Add chocolate chips and mix well. Pour into Graham Cracker Crust.

Bake 30 minutes. Let cool, then refrigerate 12 hours.

Preheat oven to 350 degrees. Spread Sour Cream Topping over top of cheesecake. Bake until set, about 30 minutes. Let cool, then refrigerate 48 hours before serving.

◆◆◆

Each serving contains about: 801 calories; 465 mg sodium; 154 mg cholesterol; 48 grams fat; 90 grams carbohydrate; 10 grams protein; 1.85 grams fiber.

DATE-NUT CHEESECAKE
The Source, Hollywood

Now closed, The Source was one of Los Angeles' first health food restaurants.

NUT CRUST:
1 cup ground almonds
1 cup ground walnuts
3 tablespoons butter, melted

FILLING:
2 cups sour cream
1 pound cream cheese, softened
1 1/2 teaspoons vanilla extract
1/2 teaspoon almond extract
3/4 cup honey
15 large pitted dates, chopped
1 1/2 cups chopped walnuts

HONEYED WHIPPED CREAM:
1 1/2 cups whipping cream
Honey

NUT CRUST:
 Preheat oven to 375 degrees. Butter 8-inch springform pan. Combine almonds and walnuts in prepared pan. Stir in melted butter and press mixture against bottom and partly up sides of pan to form crust. Bake 15 minutes to set. Let cool.

FILLING:
 Reduce oven temperature to 300 degrees. Combine sour cream, cream cheese, vanilla, almond extract and honey in bowl. Stir in dates and walnuts. Turn into Nut Crust and bake until set, about 45 minutes. Cool, then top with Honeyed Whipped Cream.

HONEYED WHIPPED CREAM:
 Whip cream and sweeten with honey to taste. Makes about 3 cups.

8 servings. Each serving contains about: 1,218 calories; 269 mg sodium; 161 mg cholesterol; 86 grams fat; 109 grams carbohydrate; 17 grams protein; 6.26 grams fiber.

ESPRESSO-MACADAMIA NUT COOKIES

Rock Restaurant, Marina del Rey

Chef Hans Rockenwagner suggests using whole nuts for maximum crunch.

4 ounces unsweetened chocolate, coarsely chopped
3 cups semisweet chocolate chips
1/2 cup (1 stick) butter
1/2 cup all-purpose flour
1/2 teaspoon baking powder
1/2 teaspoon salt
4 eggs
1 1/2 cups sugar
1 1/2 tablespoons instant espresso powder
2 teaspoons vanilla extract
50 whole macadamia nuts

Melt unsweetened chocolate, 1 1/2 cups chocolate chips and butter in top of double boiler set over, but not touching, simmering water, stirring occasionally until mixture is smooth and completely blended. Let cool to room temperature.

Sift flour, baking powder and salt into medium bowl. Set aside.

Combine eggs, sugar, espresso powder and vanilla in large bowl and beat at medium speed until mixture forms ribbon when beater is lifted, about 4 minutes. Fold in cooled chocolate mixture.

Sift half of flour mixture over top and fold in gently. Repeat with remaining flour mixture. Fold in remaining chocolate chips and macadamias. Cover batter and chill 30 minutes.

Preheat oven to 400 degrees. Grease and flour two large baking sheets. Drop 2-tablespoon mounds of batter onto prepared baking sheets, spacing at least 1 inch apart and making sure nuts are evenly distributed.

Bake until cookies are puffy and shiny, 7 to 10 minutes. Let cool on wire rack. Serve warm or at room temperature.

25 cookies. Each cookie contains about: 253 calories; 105 mg sodium; 44 mg cholesterol; 19 grams fat; 23 grams carbohydrate; 3 grams protein; 0.04 gram fiber.

HAYSTACKS

Griswold's, Claremont

Griswold's in Claremont shared this recipe with us a decade ago, and it's still a favorite with our readers.

6 1/2 cups flaked coconut
1 1/2 cups chopped dates
1 cup chopped walnuts
1/2 teaspoon salt
1 1/2 teaspoons vanilla extract
13 egg whites, lightly beaten
2 cups sugar

Combine coconut, dates, walnuts, salt and vanilla in mixing bowl. Set aside.

Combine egg whites and sugar in top of double boiler set over simmering water and cook, stirring constantly, until mixture reaches 120 degrees on candy thermometer or feels hot to touch. Pour into coconut mixture and blend well.

Preheat oven to 350 degrees. Lightly grease baking sheet. Form dough into balls with small ice cream scoop and arrange on prepared baking sheet. Bake until golden brown, about 20 minutes. Let cool, then remove from baking sheet.

◆◆◆

3 dozen cookies. Each cookie contains about: 120 calories; 67 mg sodium; 0 cholesterol; 4 grams fat; 20 grams carbohydrate; 2 grams protein; 0.45 gram fiber.

RANGER COOKIES (Flying Saucers)
Los Angeles Unified School District Cafeterias

Our readers' favorite cookie is, by far, one that was served at public schools. These Ranger Cookies (also known as Flying Saucers) are typical of the chocolate chip cookies requested by former students of the Los Angeles Unified School District.

I cup (2 sticks) butter
I cup granulated sugar
I cup brown sugar, packed
2 eggs, well beaten
2 cups sifted all-purpose flour
I teaspoon baking soda
1/2 teaspoon baking powder
1/2 teaspoon salt
I teaspoon vanilla extract
2 cups rolled oats
2 cups cornflakes
1/2 cup shredded or flaked coconut
1/2 cup semisweet chocolate chips
1/2 cup chopped walnuts

Cream butter with sugars in mixing bowl until light and fluffy. Beat in eggs.

Preheat oven to 350 degrees. Sift flour with baking soda, baking powder and salt. Blend into creamed mixture. Add vanilla, oats, cornflakes, coconut, chocolate chips and walnuts and mix until blended.

Drop 2 1/2-tablespoon mounds of dough onto ungreased baking sheets and flatten to 4-inch diameter. Bake 10 to 12 minutes. Cookies should still be slightly soft when removed from oven. Let cool briefly on baking sheets, then transfer to rack to cool completely.

About 22 large cookies. Each cookie contains about: 272 calories; 187 mg sodium; 43 mg cholesterol; 13 grams fat; 37 grams carbohydrate; 4 grams protein; 0.28 gram fiber.

KRISPY RICE SQUARES

Getty Museum Cafe, Los Angeles

When the cafeteria line at the Getty Center gets too long, the staff hands out these crispy rice squares to the patrons. The only difference between the recipe for these treats and the recipe on the cereal box or marshmallow bag is that it calls for butter instead of margarine. As a variation, try melting two peanut butter-chocolate cups along with the marshmallows.

3 tablespoons butter
10 ounces marshmallows
6 cups Rice Krispies or other puffed rice cereal

Grease 13 x 9-inch pan. Melt butter in large pot over medium heat. Add marshmallows and stir until melted. Add Rice Krispies and stir until well incorporated.

Pour into prepared pan and spread evenly. Cut into 24 squares.

24 squares. Each square contains about: 135 calories; 275 mg sodium; 4 mg cholesterol; 2 grams fat; 28 grams carbohydrate; 2 grams protein; 0.06 gram fiber.

BREAKFAST COOKIES

Julienne, San Marino

These are called "breakfast cookies" because they contain oats, brown sugar, fruit and nuts as in breakfast cereal.

3 cups rolled oats
2 cups all-purpose flour
1 cup wholewheat flour
2 cups lightly packed dark brown sugar
2 teaspoons nutmeg
1 1/2 teaspoons salt
1 1/2 teaspoons baking soda
1 cup (2 sticks) butter, softened
1 cup buttermilk
2 cups mixed chopped dried fruit and raisins
1 1/2 cups walnuts

Preheat oven to 375 degrees. Combine oats, flours, brown sugar, nutmeg, salt and baking soda. Using pastry blender or fork, cut in butter until mixture is moist and crumbly. Stir in buttermilk. Add dried fruits and walnuts. Drop by tablespoonfuls onto baking sheet and bake until browned, about 12 minutes. Let cool slightly before removing from baking sheet.

◆◆◆

About 4 dozen cookies. Each cookie contains about: 156 calories; 122 mg sodium; 11 mg cholesterol; 7 grams fat; 23 grams carbohydrate; 3 grams protein; 0.42 gram fiber.

CAFE BROWNIES

Spotlight Cafe, Music Center, Los Angeles

Readers attending performances at the Music Center raved about these brownies sold in the adjoining Spotlight Cafe kiosk. We've enjoyed them too.

10 tablespoons (1 ¼ sticks) butter
4 ounces unsweetened chocolate
5 ounces semisweet chocolate
6 eggs
2 cups sugar
1 ½ teaspoons vanilla extract
1 ⅓ cups all-purpose flour
½ teaspoon salt
4 ounces semisweet chocolate chips

Combine butter, unsweetened chocolate and semisweet chocolate in top of double boiler set over simmering water. Stir mixture constantly until thoroughly melted and smooth, about 5 minutes. Set aside.

Preheat oven to 350 degrees. Grease 13x9-inch pan. Beat eggs, sugar and vanilla at medium speed of electric mixer until fluffy, about 10 minutes. Gradually beat in flour and salt until pale in color, about 10 minutes. Add butter mixture and blend well. Stir in chocolate chips.

Pour batter into prepared pan, spreading evenly. Bake until skewer inserted in center comes out clean, about 35 minutes, rotating pan halfway through baking time.

16 brownies. Each brownie contains about: 342 calories; 173 mg sodium; 99 mg cholesterol; 20 grams fat; 41 grams carbohydrate; 5 grams protein; 0.47 gram fiber.

BANANAS and STRAWBERRIES FLAMBÉ

Bacchanal Room, Caesars Palace, Las Vegas

These flambéed bananas with strawberries were prepared with flair and flares at the table when the Bacchanal Room existed.

I tablespoon butter
2 bananas, peeled, halved lengthwise and cut in half crosswise
Juice of 1/2 lemon
2 pints strawberries, hulled and halved or sliced
I tablespoon sugar
1/2 cup orange juice
1/4 cup Cognac
6 scoops vanilla ice cream (about I pint), optional

   Melt butter in crepe pan over medium-high heat. Add bananas and sprinkle with lemon juice. Sauté until bananas are glazed but not mushy.

   Add strawberries, sugar and orange juice and cook over high heat until orange juice is almost absorbed.

   Heat Cognac until warm. Ignite. While still flaming, pour over strawberry-banana mixture. Serve with scoop of ice cream.

◆◆◆

6 servings. Each serving contains about: 130 calories; 21 mg sodium; 5 mg cholesterol; 3 grams fat; 23 grams carbohydrate; I gram protein; 2.58 grams fiber.

TARTE TATIN

Joe's Restaurant, Venice

Chef-owner Joe Miller warns that the apple syrup will make a mess while it bubbles on your stovetop. "If the spatter is cleaned up while it is still hot," he says, "the syrup will wipe right off."

15 to 18 Red Delicious apples
1 1/2 cups (3 sticks) butter
1 1/2 cups sugar
1 sheet packaged or homemade puff pastry
Whipped cream or ice cream (optional)

Peel, core and halve apples. Set aside.

Melt butter in 10-inch straight-sided skillet or sauté pan. Add sugar and melt over medium heat.

Arrange apples, rounded side up, around pan in spiral fashion. Lay any remaining apples on top of others. Cook over medium heat, shaking and spinning apples in pan to keep them from sticking. When first layer of apples has cooked until soft, squeeze remaining apples into spaces. Continue to cook until apples caramelize and turn dark brown and translucent, 40 to 45 minutes.

Preheat oven to 350 degrees. Place puff pastry sheet on work surface. Cut out circle of same diameter as pan. Lay pastry round on top of apples in skillet and bake until pastry is browned, about 20 minutes.

Remove pan from oven and invert large serving plate over pan. Invert tart right side up and remove pan. Reshape tart with spatula if necessary. Serve warm with whipped cream or ice cream.

8 servings. Each serving, without whipped cream or ice cream, contains about: 786 calories; 487 mg sodium; 93 mg cholesterol; 46 grams fat; 96 grams carbohydrate; 4 grams protein; 4.29 grams fiber.

BUTTERSCOTCH DREAM PIE

PJ's Restaurant, Cozad, Nebraska

A reader vacationing in the Midwest requested the recipe for this superb pie.

8 ounces cream cheese, softened
I cup powdered sugar
Whipped topping
1/3 cup pecan pieces
I baked 10-inch pie shell, at room temperature
1/3 cup brown sugar, packed
3 cups cold milk
2 packages (3.4 ounces each) instant butterscotch pudding mix
2 tablespoons butterscotch schnapps (optional)
I teaspoon butter, melted
Chopped pecans

Beat cream cheese with powdered sugar until smooth. Mix in 2 1/2 cups whipped topping. Sprinkle pecan pieces into pie shell. Spread cream cheese mixture in shell.

Mix brown sugar and cold milk until sugar is dissolved. Add pudding mix, stirring with wire whisk until smooth and starting to thicken. Mix according to package directions. Add butterscotch schnapps and butter and mix well.

Let stand up to 5 minutes or until almost but not completely set, with whisk indentations remaining somewhat visible. Carefully pour on top of cream cheese mixture, spreading evenly. Chill until set.

Spread 1/4 to 1/2 inch of whipped topping on top of pudding, or pipe whipped topping from pastry tube in dollops or circle around edge of pie. Garnish with sprinkling of chopped pecans.

◆◆◆

10 servings. Each serving contains about: 469 calories; 226 mg sodium; 31 mg cholesterol; 26 grams fat; 57 grams carbohydrate; 6 grams protein; 0.10 gram fiber.

TRUCK STOP REECE PIE

P&H Truck Stop, Wells River, Vermont

"Reece" refers to the pie's flavor resemblance to Reese's, the peanut butter-chocolate cups. P&H Truck Stop, an oasis for truckers and travelers in Wells River, Vermont, is famous for this pie. Numerous copycat versions circulate.

3/4 cup plus 3 tablespoons powdered sugar
1/2 cup peanut butter
1 9-inch baked or graham cracker pie shell
1 package (5 1/8 ounces) chocolate pudding mix
3 cups milk
2 tablespoons unsweetened cocoa powder
1/2 cup whipping cream, whipped
Chocolate sprinkles (optional)

Combine 3/4 cup powdered sugar and peanut butter in bowl, mixing well. Spread over bottom of pie shell, reserving 2 tablespoons for topping. If mixture is too stiff to spread, add small amount of warm water.

Prepare chocolate pudding according to package directions, using milk. Pour over peanut butter layer in pie crust. Chill.

Sift cocoa into whipped cream and swirl. Spread over cooled pie. Add remaining 3 tablespoons powdered sugar to reserved peanut butter topping and sprinkle over pie. Garnish with chocolate sprinkles.

◆◆◆

6 servings. Each serving contains about: 644 calories; 245 mg sodium; 37 mg cholesterol; 38 grams fat; 67 grams carbohydrate; 13 grams protein; 0.7 gram fiber.

TIRAMISÙ
Boccaccio, Westlake Village

Tiramisù — "pick me up" in Italian — is said to have been invented by a brothel cook in the northern regions, bent on giving the staff a lift before a long, hard night's work. The Italian biscotti and cream dessert became a rage here in the late 1970s, and now you'll find tiramisù in Italian restaurants, supermarkets and bakeries everywhere. It's not as difficult to prepare as you might think.

8 eggs, separated
2 1/4 cups powdered sugar
1 pound plus 2 ounces mascarpone cheese
1 1/2 cups brewed espresso
1/4 cup amaretto
1 package (3 ounces) ladyfingers, split lengthwise

Beat egg yolks with powdered sugar at medium speed of electric mixer until pale and creamy, about 5 minutes. Add mascarpone and beat until thick and firm.

Using clean beaters, whip egg whites until fluffy and firm, 3 to 4 minutes. Fold into mascarpone mixture.

Combine espresso and amaretto. Quickly dip ladyfinger halves in espresso mixture on each side. Arrange layer of ladyfingers in bottom of 9-inch square dish. Spread with half of mascarpone mixture. Dip remaining ladyfingers in espresso mixture and layer in dish; spread remaining mascarpone on top. Chill 2 hours.

◆◆◆

8 servings. Each serving contains about: 474 calories; 261 mg sodium; 320 mg cholesterol; 28 grams fat; 42 grams carbohydrate; 12 grams protein; 0.01 gram fiber.

❖ *Chef's Tip*: See page 92 for tips on cooking with raw eggs.

KEY LIME PIE

Cafe del Sol, Marriott Marco Island Resort, Florida

Key limes produce a sharper taste than other limes; they're the same as the yellow limes you sometimes find in Mexican markets and some gourmet stores. But even if you use everyday green limes, this pie is delicious.

PECAN CRUST:
1 tablespoon butter
1 1/2 cups chopped pecans
3/4 cup graham cracker crumbs
Grated peel of 2 limes
3/4 teaspoon cinnamon
1 1/2 tablespoons sugar

FILLING:
7 egg yolks
2 cans (14 ounces each) sweetened condensed milk
1/2 cup Key lime or other lime juice
Grated peel of 2 limes
Whipped cream

PECAN CRUST:
Melt butter in medium skillet. Add pecans and sauté until lightly browned. Immediately transfer nuts and butter to food processor. Add crumbs, lime peel, cinnamon and sugar and blend to form coarse crumbs. Turn into 10-inch pie plate, reserving 1/4 cup of crumbs for garnish. Evenly distribute crumb mixture over bottom and sides of pie plate, pressing to cover surface. Let stand at room temperature until ready to fill.

FILLING:
Preheat oven to 300 degrees. Beat egg yolks at high speed until smooth, 4 to 5 minutes. Slowly blend in condensed milk; do not overmix. Scrape down sides of bowl. Gradually add lime juice, beating at medium speed. Add peel and mix slowly.
Pour into prepared Pecan Crust, smoothing top with rubber spatula. Fill baking pan halfway with hot water and place on lowest oven rack. Place pie plate on rack

above water and bake until filling is firm to touch, 20 to 25 minutes. Do not allow pie to brown.

Let pie cool to room temperature on wire rack, then refrigerate to set and chill, about 4 hours.

To serve, top pie with 3/4-inch-thick layer of whipped cream and sprinkle with reserved graham cracker crumb mixture.

◆◆◆

8 servings. Each serving contains about: 535 calories; 202 mg sodium; 276 mg cholesterol; 26 grams fat; 68 grams carbohydrate; 12 grams protein; 0.35 gram fiber.

COCONUT BANANA CREAM PIE
Lawry's Prime Rib, Los Angeles

Lawry's has graciously shared many good recipes with our readers over the years. This one is among them.

COCONUT PIE SHELL:
1/2 cup (I stick) butter
3 cups flaked coconut

FILLING:
4 egg yolks
3/4 cup sugar
3 tablespoons cornstarch
1/4 teaspoon salt
1/4 cup all-purpose flour
3 cups half and half
2 drops yellow food coloring
2 teaspoons vanilla extract
2 bananas
I cup heavy whipping cream
I tablespoon powdered sugar

COCONUT PIE SHELL:
    Lightly butter 9-inch pie plate. Melt 1/2 cup butter in large skillet and sauté coconut, stirring constantly, until golden brown, about 5 minutes. Press firmly and evenly into prepared pie plate to form shell. Chill while preparing filling.

FILLING:
    Combine egg yolks, 1/4 cup sugar, cornstarch, salt and flour in small bowl. Gradually add I cup half and half.
    Combine remaining 2 cups half and half and 1/2 cup sugar in 3-quart saucepan and bring just to boil over medium heat. Add egg mixture and cook and stir until mixture returns to boil and thickens, about I minute.
    Remove from heat. Stir in food coloring and vanilla. Cover surface with plastic wrap to prevent skin from forming. Let cool.

Peel and slice bananas into Coconut Pie Shell. Pour filling into shell.

Whip cream with powdered sugar until stiff. Spoon in dollops or pipe with pastry bag around edge of pie. Chill 2 hours before slicing.

◆◆◆

8 servings. Each serving contains about: 655 calories; 335 mg sodium; 242 mg cholesterol; 48 grams fat; 53 grams carbohydrate; 6 grams protein; 0.92 gram fiber.

CUSTARD and CROISSANT PUDDING
Patina, Los Angeles

This is bread pudding so grand you'll want to serve it for Thanksgiving or other special parties.

WILD TURKEY SAUCE:
5 egg yolks
5 tablespoons sugar
1 cup milk
1 cup whipping cream
2 to 4 tablespoons Wild Turkey bourbon

PUDDING:
10 egg yolks
3/4 cup sugar
1 vanilla bean
4 cups whipping cream or half and half
1 croissant, cubed and toasted
1 1/2 ounces good-quality semisweet chocolate, chopped

WILD TURKEY SAUCE:
Blend egg yolks and sugar in small bowl. Combine milk and cream in saucepan and bring to boil. Remove from heat and stir in sugar mixture. Cook over low heat until sauce thickens, about 10 to 15 minutes; do not boil. Stir in Wild Turkey to taste. Let cool, then chill. Makes 2 cups.

PUDDING:
Beat yolks with sugar until pale in color. Add vanilla bean and cream. Set aside.

Preheat oven to 300 degrees. Divide croissant cubes and chocolate evenly among 8 individual soufflé dishes. Remove vanilla bean and pour custard over croissant and chocolate.

Arrange dishes in roasting pan half filled with hot water. Bake 45 minutes or until firm (croissant and chocolate will rise to surface). Serve at room temperature with Wild Turkey Sauce.

8 servings. Each serving contains about: 900 calories; 110 mg sodium; 608 mg cholesterol; 68 grams fat; 64 grams carbohydrate; 10 grams protein; 0.18 gram fiber.

GINGER CRÈME BRÛLÉE

Chaya Venice, Venice

As soon as they tried this, our tasters were as thrilled as the readers who requested the recipe. And it's so easy!

Peeled fresh ginger
6 egg yolks
1 1/3 cups heavy whipping cream
1/4 cup milk
1/2 cup plus 2 tablespoons sugar
1 tablespoon vanilla extract

   Set fine metal grater or Japanese porcelain ginger grater over small bowl and grate enough ginger to collect 2 teaspoons juice in bowl (freezing ginger makes grating easier). Set aside.

   Preheat oven to 300 degrees. Combine egg yolks, cream, milk, 1/2 cup sugar, vanilla and ginger juice in bowl and blend well. Pour into six 3-ounce custard cups. Arrange cups in baking dish 1/4 filled with boiling water. Bake 25 to 30 minutes or until custard is set; do not overcook.

   Preheat broiler. Sprinkle 1 teaspoon sugar over each custard and place under broiler to lightly brown and caramelize surface; do not scorch. Chill before serving.

◆◆◆

6 servings. Each serving contains about: 333 calories; 34 mg sodium; 346 mg cholesterol; 25 grams fat; 23 grams carbohydrate; 4 grams protein; 0 fiber.

CREMA CATALANA

La Paella, Los Angeles

Crema Catalana is the Spanish version of crème brûlée, and La Paella's is as good as any we've had in Spain.

1/2 cup cornstarch
4 cups milk
1 stick cinnamon
Zest of 1/2 lemon, in one piece
6 egg yolks
1 1/4 cups sugar

Dissolve cornstarch in 1 cup milk. Set aside.

Heat remaining milk, cinnamon stick and lemon zest in saucepan over medium heat until boiling, about 5 minutes. Set aside and let cool about 10 minutes.

Mix yolks and 1 cup sugar in medium bowl. Strain boiled milk into yolk mixture. Add dissolved cornstarch mixture and blend well. Pour into clean saucepan and simmer over low heat, stirring constantly, until thickened, about 2 to 3 minutes. Remove from heat and strain again through fine sieve.

Divide custard among six individual ovenproof dishes. Refrigerate at least 2 hours.

Just before serving, turn on oven broiler. Spread remaining 1/4 cup sugar to evenly cover custards. Set dishes on rack beneath broiler and broil until sugar bubbles and browns, about 1 minute.

◆◆◆

6 servings. Each serving contains about: 346 calories; 91 mg sodium; 285 mg cholesterol; 9 grams fat; 60 grams carbohydrate; 8 grams protein; 0.01 gram fiber.

CHOCOLATE SOUFFLÉ

Moustache Cafe, Hollywood

The dollop of whipped cream sunk into the steaming center gives the soufflé a wonderful finish.

7 ounces unsweetened chocolate
1/2 cup milk
Sugar
4 egg yolks
6 egg whites
Butter
Powdered sugar
Whipped cream (optional)

Combine unsweetened chocolate, milk and 7 tablespoons sugar in top of double boiler over simmering water. Cook, stirring occasionally, until chocolate and sugar are melted. Remove from heat and let stand 10 minutes.

Whisk in egg yolks until well blended.

In mixing bowl, beat egg whites until stiff. Add 1 tablespoon sugar and continue beating until blended. With wire whisk, stir 1/2 of egg white mixture into chocolate mixture. Gently fold in remaining egg whites.

Preheat oven to 350 degrees. Butter entire inside surface and rims of six individual soufflé dishes and sprinkle with granulated sugar. Fill each soufflé dish to rim with chocolate mixture. Bake until set, about 20 minutes.

Remove from oven, dust with powdered sugar and serve immediately with a dollop of whipped cream, if desired.

6 servings. Each serving, without cream, contains about: 347 calories; 66 mg sodium; 183 mg cholesterol; 20 grams fat; 36 grams carbohydrate; 11 grams protein; 0 fiber.

CAPIROTADA

Sonora Cafe, Hollywood

This is a multi-part recipe. To avoid kitchen battle fatigue, take a tip from television cooks who prepare such dishes in stages and assemble the parts at the last moment. The sauce, filling and custard can be prepared separately days ahead.

APRICOT FILLING:
2 cups sugar
1 cup water
1/2 cup dried apricots

BUTTERSCOTCH SAUCE:
1 1/2 cups brown sugar, packed
1/4 cup water
6 tablespoons butter
1 1/2 cups whipping cream
1 tablespoon cider vinegar

CUSTARD FILLING:
6 eggs
4 cups whipping cream
1/2 cup sugar
2/3 cup all-purpose flour
1 large loaf brioche or French bread
1 Golden Delicious apple, cored, peeled and shredded
1/2 cup raisins
Whipped cream

APRICOT FILLING:
Bring sugar and water to boil. Add dried apricots. Reduce heat to medium-low and simmer until apricots are soft, about 20 minutes. Let apricots cool in syrup. Drain apricots and chop.

BUTTERSCOTCH SAUCE:

Combine brown sugar and water in 3-quart saucepan and stir over low heat until sugar dissolves, about 2 minutes. Increase heat and bring mixture to boil. Remove from heat and cool 5 minutes.

Return sauce to medium-low heat. Gradually stir in butter until mixture reaches rolling boil; boil 2 minutes. Add cream and vinegar, stirring constantly. Boil 1 minute longer. Set aside.

CUSTARD FILLING:

Beat eggs in bowl. Mix in cream, sugar and flour. Refrigerate until ready to use.

Preheat oven to 325 degrees. Trim crusts from bread. Cut bread into 1/2-inch-thick slices. Layer 1/3 of bread slices on bottom of 13 x 9-inch glass baking dish, covering bottom completely; do not overlap bread slices. Sprinkle half of apple, 1/4 cup raisins and half of Apricot Filling over bread. Pour 1/3 of Butterscotch Sauce over fruit. Top with half of Custard Filling. Place another 1/3 of bread slices over fruit-custard mixture. Top with remaining apple, raisins and Apricot Filling, then 1/3 of Butterscotch Sauce and remaining Custard Filling. Arrange last of bread over top to cover. Top with remaining Butterscotch Sauce.

Bake until custard is set and skewer inserted in center comes out clean, about 1 hour. If pudding browns too quickly, cover loosely with foil and continue baking. Let cool 20 minutes. Serve warm with whipped cream.

◆◆◆

12 servings. Each serving contains about: 731 calories; 138 mg sodium; 273 mg cholesterol; 49 grams fat; 71 grams carbohydrate; 6 grams protein; 0.18 gram fiber.

CREMA di VANIGLIA (Vanilla Cream)

Il Moro, West Los Angeles

This rich Italian custard is one of my personal favorites.

10 egg yolks
3/4 cup sugar
1/2 cup milk
I quart whipping cream
I teaspoon vanilla extract

Beat egg yolks and sugar until creamy. Stir in milk, cream and vanilla. Refrigerate until chilled, about 2 hours. Skim foam off surface.

Preheat oven to 350 degrees. Pour custard into eight 6-ounce custard cups. Arrange in 13 x 9-inch baking pan half filled with hot water. Cover entire pan with foil; pierce foil in several places to allow steam to escape. Bake until set, about I hour.

Remove foil and cool custards I hour, then refrigerate at least 2 hours before serving.

8 servings. Each serving contains about: 572 calories; 63 mg sodium; 506 mg cholesterol; 52 grams fat; 23 grams carbohydrate; 6 grams protein; 0 fiber.

DEEP CHOCOLATE PUDDING

Vince & Eddie's, New York City

Here's a classy chocolate pudding, garnished with mint and hazelnuts, that Grandma would probably never dream of.

PUDDING:

1 quart milk
1/3 cup unsweetened cocoa powder
1/2 cup sugar
Pinch of salt
1/4 cup cornstarch
13 ounces bittersweet chocolate, melted
1/4 cup (1/2 stick) unsalted butter, melted
2 tablespoons vanilla extract
1 tablespoon chopped hazelnuts
6 sprigs mint

WHIPPED CREAM:

1/3 cup heavy whipping cream
1/2 teaspoon vanilla extract
1 tablespoon powdered sugar

PUDDING:

Combine milk, cocoa, sugar, salt and cornstarch in medium saucepan and bring to simmer. Cook, stirring constantly, until thickened. Combine chocolate, butter and vanilla in bowl. Pour milk mixture into chocolate mixture and blend well. Pour through fine strainer. Divide mixture among six glasses. Refrigerate until cold. Top each pudding with Whipped Cream and garnish with nuts and mint sprigs.

WHIPPED CREAM:

In bowl, whip cream with vanilla and powdered sugar until stiff.

6 servings. Each serving contains about: 403 calories; 129 mg sodium; 51 mg cholesterol; 25 grams fat; 43 grams carbohydrate; 8 grams protein; 0.70 gram fiber.

CHOCOLATE TART

Rockenwagner, Santa Monica

Roll up your sleeves. It's going to be a cooking feat you'll remember for a long time—but worth it.

COFFEE CRÈME ANGLAISE:

5 egg yolks
1/2 cup sugar
1 pint whipping cream or half and half
2 teaspoons finely ground coffee beans

ORANGE CONFIT:

1 orange
1/2 cup sugar
1/4 cup water
1 tablespoon light corn syrup

CHOCOLATE FILLING:

9 ounces fine semisweet Belgian, French or Swiss chocolate (preferably Valrhona or
    Callebaut), coarsely chopped
1/2 cup (1 stick) butter
Pinch of salt
6 egg yolks
Scant 1/3 cup sugar
2 egg whites
6 strawberries, sliced and fanned
6 sprigs mint
Powdered sugar

COFFEE CRÈME ANGLAISE:

In bowl of electric mixer beat egg yolks and sugar until mixture is pale yellow and forms ribbon when beaters are lifted. Set aside.

Place medium-size bowl into larger bowl of ice; set aside. In medium saucepan over medium heat, bring cream just to boil, stirring. Remove from heat and stir in coffee. Add half of hot cream to egg mixture, beating with mixer, then return entire mixture to remaining cream. Place over low heat and cook, stirring constantly, until sauce thickens and coats back of metal spoon; do not boil. Immediately pour hot sauce into bowl set over ice and stir to prevent further cooking or curdling. If lumps develop, strain sauce through fine sieve. Refrigerate up to 24 hours before use.

ORANGE CONFIT:

Using sharp swivel-bladed vegetable peeler, remove orange zest in pieces, then trim any white pith from back of each strip. Cut strips into 1/8-inch widths. Cover zest with cold water in small saucepan and bring to boil. Drain. Return zest to pan and again cover with cold water. Bring to boil. Drain and repeat process, this time draining on paper towels (this is called "triple blanching").

In clean saucepan combine sugar, water and corn syrup and stir gently over low heat until sugar dissolves. Add blanched orange zest and bring to simmer; simmer until orange peel is tender, about 7 to 10 minutes. Store confit, covered, in glass or ceramic bowl or jar in refrigerator until ready to serve, up to 1 week.

CHOCOLATE FILLING:

Butter and flour six individual 4-inch tart pans. Combine chocolate and butter in top of double boiler or large heatproof bowl over gently simmering water. Add salt and heat, stirring occasionally, until mixture is well blended and smooth. Let chocolate mixture cool slightly.

Using electric mixer, beat egg yolks and about 1/4 cup sugar at high speed until mixture forms ribbon when beaters are lifted. Using rubber spatula, fold egg yolk mixture into warm chocolate mixture.

Using clean, dry beaters, beat egg whites with remaining sugar until stiff peaks form. Fold 1/3 of egg white mixture into chocolate mixture. Gently fold remaining egg whites into chocolate mixture, blending evenly but lightly. Pour into prepared tart pans, filling to within 1/2 inch of top. Arrange tarts on tray and cover with plastic wrap. Refrigerate up to 6 hours.

Shortly before serving, preheat oven to 400 degrees. Arrange tarts on baking sheet and bake until tops appear cracked and cakelike but tarts remain runny inside, 8 to 10 minutes. Holding each tart pan in one hand with oven mitt, loosen tart with sharp knife and turn out onto one side of dessert plate.

Spoon pool of Coffee Crème Anglaise onto opposite side of plate. Slice and fan strawberry and place next to sauce on each plate. Dot Orange Confit on top of each tart. Garnish each tart with mint sprig, and sift a little powdered sugar over entire dessert. Serve at once.

◆◆◆

6 individual tarts. Each tart contains about: 985 calories; 260 mg sodium; 650 mg cholesterol; 71 grams fat; 87 grams carbohydrate; 11 grams protein; 1.31 grams fiber.

INDEX

♦♦♦

OTHER BOOKS FROM THE LOS ANGELES TIMES

SOS RECIPES: 30 YEARS OF REQUESTS
By Rose Dosti
This best selling book offers hundreds of tried-and true recipes for all-time favorite dishes that literally range from soup to nuts.
$19.45

MODERN CALIFORNIA COOKING
More than 300 recipes, hand picked by the Times' food staff, celebrate California's fresh and flavorful style of cooking.
$22.45

LOW FAT KITCHEN
By Donna Deane
Scores of recipes that use fresh food flavor, not fat, to satisfy your taste buds.
$20.45

DRAWING THE LINE
By Paul Conrad
Two hundred drawings, spanning the period from the late 1960s to President Clinton's impeachment trial, from America's premier political cartoonist.
$24.45

IMAGINING LOS ANGELES
PHOTOGRAPHS OF A 20TH CENTURY CITY
More than 175 photos tell the story of Los Angeles' coming of age in the 20th Century. With a foreword by celebrated author Ray Bradbury.
$28.95

52 WEEKS IN THE CALIFORNIA GARDEN
By Robert Smaus
How to make the most of your garden by the foremost authority on gardening in California.
$17.45

CURBSIDE LA
AN OFFBEAT GUIDE TO THE CITY OF ANGELS
By Cecilia Rasmussen
Enjoy a truly eclectic tour of Los Angeles with enticing excursions into the city's peerless history and diversity.
$19.45

L.A. UNCONVENTIONAL
By Cecilia Rasmussen
Where some people see roadblocks, others, such as the men and women in this volume, see possibility, opportunity and excitement.
$30.95

ETERNALLY YOURS
By Jack Smith
When longtime Times' columnist Jack Smith died in 1996, his widow, Denise, and two sons, Curt and Doug, collected some of their favorite columnists for this treasured volume.
$16.95

LAST OF THE BEST
90 COLUMNS FROM THE 1990S BY THE LATE JIM MURRAY
The best of Jim's columns from the last decade of his life. Foreword by Dodger legend Tommy Lasorda.
$19.45

THE GREAT ONES
By Jim Murray
The top men and women of the sports world written about as only this late, great sports columnist could. Foreword by Arnold Palmer.
$22.45

To order, call (800) 246-4042 or visit our web site at
http://www.latimes.com/bookstore